# INSIDE THE
# COLD WAR

YA
909.82
WAR

**This edition published in 2019 by:**
The Rosen Publishing Group, Inc.
29 East 21st Street
New York, NY 10010

Additional end matter copyright © 2019 by The Rosen Publishing Group, Inc.

### Cataloging-in-Publication Data

Names: Ware, Pat.
Title: Inside the Cold War / Pat Ware.
Description: New York : Rosen YA, 2019. | Series: The geek's guide to espionage and warfare | Includes abbreviations and glossary.
Identifiers: ISBN 9781508186144 (pbk.) | ISBN 9781499467673 (library bound)
Subjects: LCSH: Cold War—Juvenile literature. | World politics—1945–1989—Juvenile literature. | United States—Foreign relations—1945–1989—Juvenile literature. | United States—Politics and government—1945–1989—Juvenile literature.
Classification: LCC E744.W37 2019 | DDC 909.82'5—dc23

*Manufactured in the United States of America*

Originally published in English by Haynes Publishing under the title:
Cold War Operations manual © Pat Ware 2016.

# INSIDE THE
# COLD WAR

PAT WARE

Rosen
**YA**
New York

# Contents

FALLOUT SHELTER

"I do not believe that civilization will be wiped out in a war fought with the atomic bomb. Perhaps two-thirds of the people of the earth will be killed."

Albert Einstein, 1879–1955

# Introduction

The expression "Cold War" describes a period of military and political tension between East and West that existed from 1946 to 1991. Although the term had first been used by George Orwell in an article entitled "You and the Atom Bomb" published in the *Tribune* in October 1945, it entered the common culture following a speech given by the American statesman Bernard Baruch.

Addressing the South Carolina House of Representatives in April 1947, Baruch said "Let us not be deceived ... we are today in the midst of a cold war ... our enemies are to be found abroad and at home ... let us never forget this ... our unrest is the heart of their success. The peace of the world is the hope and the goal of our political system ... it is the despair and defeat of those who stand against us."

Six months later, at a Senate Special Committee investigating the National Defense Program, Baruch returned to the theme, stating that "although the shooting war is over, we are in the midst of a cold war which is getting warmer." On one side of this Cold War were the Western powers that would form the North Atlantic Treaty Organization (NATO); on the other was the Soviet Union and the satellite states of the Warsaw Pact.

**OPPOSITE** "Polaris" ICBM fired from the submerged Royal Navy submarine HMS *Revenge*, 1983. *(US Department of Defense)*

**BELOW** Distinctive mushroom cloud and waterspout resulting from the underwater detonation of a 23-kiloton atomic bomb code-named "Helen of Bikini"; July 1946, Bikini Atoll. *(US Department of Defense)*

an "Iron Curtain" separated East and West. In June 1948, the Soviets blocked access to the Western-controlled areas of Berlin in an attempt to bring the entire city under Soviet control. A huge Allied airlift was established, delivering 300 tons (270 tonnes) of food, fuel and other necessities every day into Berlin Tempelhof airport. The West's determination ensured that the Soviet gamble failed and, in May 1949, the blockade was lifted, and Germany was divided into two separate states with competing ideologies – the German Democratic Republic (GDR) in the east, and the Federal Republic of Germany (DDR) in the west.

In August 1949, the Soviet Union carried out its first test of a fission device, breaking the US monopoly in atomic weapons and heralding the beginning of the nuclear arms race. Not long after, Britain also joined the "nuclear club," although it was often difficult to separate the nation's "independent nuclear deterrent" from the arsenal of "the American cousins." Other nations, including China, France, India, Pakistan, Israel and North Korea have subsequently developed nuclear weapons.

**ABOVE The Berlin Wall, constructed during 1961, came to signify the divide between East and West. This photograph was taken at the junction of Elsen Strasse and Heidelberger Strasse in the American sector.** *(Warehouse Collection)*

The Cold War brought an end to the uneasy alliance that had seen the Soviet Union join with Britain, Canada and the USA in 1941 to defeat Germany and Japan. Cracks in the alliance had started to emerge in May 1945, following the German surrender, and were exacerbated by the USA's use of atomic weapons in Japan. The Soviet Union consolidated its hold over East Germany and over countries such as Poland, Hungary and Czechoslovakia, and soon

In 1950, in a pamphlet entitled "Survival under Atomic Attack," the US government stated that "atomic weapons will not destroy the earth … not even hydrogen bombs will blow the earth apart or kill us all by radioactivity." Nevertheless, during three decades, the two sides struggled to acquire nuclear supremacy. Despite attempts at reaching agreement on arms control, ever-more monstrous sums of money were committed to the acquisition of weapons that could destroy civilization many times over. Similar sums were devoted to espionage, to so-called "early warning" systems, and to devising and building the insane infrastructure required to support the very notion of nuclear war.

For 50 years, the world stood uneasily on the edge of nuclear warfare, with few doubting that, should the Cold War turn hot, neither side could emerge victorious. The first bit of light came in the mid to late 1980s, when, in an attempt to control military expenditure, President Gorbachev refused to commit Soviet troops to support the failing Warsaw Pact regimes in Eastern Europe. A wave of revolutions saw the old order overturned in one Soviet bloc country after another, including the GDR, and,

**RIGHT Operation Buster Jangle was a series of seven nuclear tests conducted at the Nevada Test Site in 1951. The largest weapon was a 31-kiloton bomb, code-named 'Dog', whilst 'Charlie', seen here, yielded 14 kilotons.** *(US National Nuclear Security Administration)*

LEFT For some 20 years, the V-Bomber force, comprising the Avro Vulcan, seen here in the distinctive anti-flash white paint, together with the Valiant and Victor, provided Britain's strategic nuclear strike force. *(Ministry of Defence)*

BELOW Domestic fallout shelters were always considered too expensive by the UK government, although this issue was taken much more seriously in the US. This photograph shows a "typical" American family, safe in their brick-built shelter, waiting for the all-clear on the radio. *(US Department of Defense)*

on October 3, 1990, East and West Germany were unified. Within three weeks 22 nations had signed the Conventional Forces in Europe Treaty, limiting the numbers of troops and weapons that could be held by the two sides in Europe. In December 1991, following a power struggle in Moscow, the Soviet Union collapsed.

Most historians would agree that the Cold War was now well and truly over.

Nevertheless, even 25 years later, the Cold War, along with the very real, though curiously farcical, threat of nuclear apocalypse, remains a potent force in popular culture, and, of course, the worldwide nuclear stockpiles also remain – diminished, but more than capable of destroying civilization. It seems that the world must continue to "live under the shadow of the bomb."

*Chapter One*

# The Cold War story

Although it symbolizes the military tensions of the nuclear age, the Cold War was primarily a conflict of ideologies rather than weapons. The technology simply provided a measure of the competition between the two sides. However, the fear of unleashing the nuclear apocalypse – a possible complete or near-complete annihilation of life on the planet by the use of a large enough quantity of nuclear weapons – almost certainly prevented the two sides engaging one another.

**OPPOSITE** The ruins of Nagasaki Temple photographed in September 1946, some six weeks after the attack on the city. *(Corporal Lynn P. Walker, Jr; US Department of Defense)*

**RIGHT** US War Department memo, dated July 25, 1945, authorizing the use of an atomic bomb – described as a "special bomb" – on the cities of Hiroshima, Kokura, Niigata or Nagasaki. *(US National Archives)*

**BELOW** Crew of the "Enola Gay," photographed on August 5, 1945. Pilot Paul Tibbets is in the center. *(US Department of Defense)*

**BELOW RIGHT** The first nuclear weapon to be deployed, seen here at Tinian Island before being loaded on to the "Enola Gay" for delivery to Nagasaki, was a uranium-based device code-named "Little Boy." *(US Department of Defense)*

The world awoke to the realities of the nuclear age on August 6, 1945, when a lone B-29 Superfortress bomber of the US Army Air Force, piloted by Paul Tibbets and Robert Lewis, and named "Enola Gay" in dubious honor of Tibbets's mother, dropped a primitive atomic bomb on the Japanese port city of Hiroshima. The target was selected on the basis that it had not been previously bombed, and thus it would be easier to assess the scale of damage. The B-29 took off from Tinian Island, approximately 1,500 miles (2,430 km) south of Tokyo, and approached

the city at a height of 30,000 feet (9,150 m). Releasing the bomb 2 miles (3 km) short of the target, the aircraft immediately veered away, returning at a height of 28,500 feet (8,695 m). A handwritten note on the pilot's flight log, which was recently offered for sale at auction, warned that the aircraft must "stay at least 2–3 miles from the atomic cloud at all times."

For maximum destructive effect, the 15-kiloton fission bomb, code-named "Little Boy," was exploded at a height of less than 2,000 feet (655 m). The bomb contained about 140 pounds (64 kg) of enriched uranium, an extremely dense, purple-black metal. Despite the fact that only a tiny proportion of this material actually fissioned, the temperature on the ground directly beneath the blast reached 10,000°F (5,500°C), and a cloud of debris rose 11 miles (18 km) into the air. One square mile of the city was wiped out, and 90% of buildings were destroyed within a radius of 4.4 square miles (11 km²). Firefighting was rendered impossible by the fact that 26 out of 33 fire stations were destroyed; water, electricity and gas utilities were severely disrupted, and all of the city's hospitals were damaged. Glass was broken at a distance of almost 8 miles (13 km) from the center of the explosion.

The fact that the bomb was released by a lone aircraft had the effect of increasing the death toll; the aircraft was not determined to be a threat and the city's air-raid warning was cancelled. Of the city's population of around 300,000, the

**ABOVE** Mushroom cloud photographed by the tail-gunner of "Enola Gay," Staff-Sergeant George R. (Bob) Caron, at 20,000 feet (6,100 m) above Hiroshima after the dropping of "Little Boy." *(US National Archives)*

**ABOVE RIGHT** Hiroshima, after the bomb. *(US Department of Defense)*

authorities estimated that around one-quarter were killed immediately by the initial explosion and the ensuing wave of intense heat, whilst a similar number were injured. The overall casualty figure included 260 doctors out of a total of 300, 1,800 nurses out of 2,400 and some 80% of the firemen on duty. Deaths from the effects of radiation continued for many years after.

Making an entry in his log on his return from the mission, co-pilot Captain Robert Lewis wrote: "My God, what have we done," and one contemporary journal described the bomb as "the world's most terrifying weapon." Not

**RIGHT** Now described as the Hiroshima Peace Memorial or the Genbaku Dome, the ruins of the Hiroshima Prefectural Industrial Promotion Hall survive to this day as a monument to those who died at Hiroshima. *(Frank 'Fg2' Gualtieri)*

ABOVE Mushroom cloud over Nagasaki as a result of the detonation of "Fat Man," the second atomic bomb. The name was a reference to the bomb's distinctive rounded shape. *(US National Archives)*

BELOW Atomic cloud over Nagasaki, seen from neighboring Koyagi-jima Island; August 9, 1945. *(Hiromichi Matsuda)*

everyone shared Lewis's horror. For example, Henry Stimson, US Secretary of War, said that the bomb had been intended to "make a profound psychological impression on as many inhabitants [of Japan] as possible." President Harry S. Truman described it as the "bomb to end bombs," and made the following public announcement after the raid: "Sixteen hours ago an American airplane dropped one bomb on Hiroshima, Japan. That bomb had more power than 20,000 tons (18,000 tonnes) of TNT and more than 2,000 times the blast power of the British 'grand slam,' which [at 22,000 pounds] is the largest bomb yet used in the history of warfare." Speaking after the event, General Carl Spaatz, US Commander of the Strategic Air Forces in the Pacific, told journalists that he believed that had the "new bomb" been developed earlier it would have shortened the war in Europe, and may even have obviated the need for the D-Day invasion and the slog across France into Germany.

But the Japanese failed to surrender immediately, apparently refusing to believe that the USA had constructed a nuclear bomb, or, if such a feat had been achieved, that there could not have been more than a single weapon available. Three days later, on August 9, 1945, a second nuclear device, code-named "Fat Man" in reference to its rounded shape, was dropped on Nagasaki. The original target had been Kitakyushu, but the city was obscured by heavy cloud, and the lone Superfortress, nicknamed "Bockscar" after its usual pilot, Captain Frederick C. Bock, was diverted to Nagasaki. The pilot given the dubious honor of carrying out this particular mission was Major Charles W. Sweeney.

"Fat Man" had a yield of 21 kilotons, and was based on plutonium-239, using an implosion technology. The bomb was detonated 1,625 feet (500 m) directly above a suburb that included factories, housing and schools, destroying 2.6 square miles (6.7 m²) of the city; 23% of the city's 51,000 buildings were either razed to the ground by blast, or were burned. The harbor and the residential areas escaped serious damage, but the huge Mitsubishi factory in the Urakami Valley was destroyed. There was no firestorm, but the column of smoke and debris could be seen more than 250 miles (405 km) away. Of the city's population of around 270,000, the Committee on Damage by Atomic Bombs in Hiroshima and Nagasaki estimated that 75,000 were killed immediately by the initial explosion and intense heat, while a further 75,000 were injured.

The Americans believed that, within two weeks, they would be in a position to drop a third bomb on Japan, with the cities of Osaka, Nagoya and Yokosuka listed as possible targets. However, Japan surrendered unconditionally on August 15, signalling the end of the Second World War.

## Nuclear weapon development

The notion of nuclear weapons was not new. As early as 1902, two British scientists, Ernest Rutherford, a Scottish Calvinist, and Professor Frederick Soddy, had concluded that atoms contained enormous stores of energy and that, if harnessed, this energy could be used as a formidable weapon. By 1920, scientists had deduced that such a weapon could be based on the fusion of light atoms or the fission – breaking apart – of heavy atoms, and in 1932, James Chadwick, who had been a pupil of Rutherford, discovered the neutron, demonstrating how it could easily be used to penetrate atomic nuclei. Two years later, German chemists Otto Hahn and Fritz Strassmann investigated the effects of bombarding uranium-235, the most complex of the naturally occurring elements, with neutrons. By the end of 1938, Hahn reported in the science journal *Naturwissenschaften* that, under bombardment, the nucleus could be seen to "burst" or fission and that this produced new elements, including barium, krypton and strontium, plus a very large amount of energy. Clearly, if a chain reaction could be created, then the amount of energy released would be considerable – and if enough uranium were used then it would be possible to harness this energy to produce a bomb with huge destructive power.

A major problem was the availability of sufficient uranium-235, as tons of ore, in the form of pitchblende, were required to produce just a small quantity. The more common

isotope, uranium-238, contains about 0.75% uranium-235 and centrifuges were used to separate out the lighter material. Using the still secret man-made element plutonium-239 was similarly difficult, since the material had to be created in a nuclear reactor.

ABOVE "Fat Man" on its transport carriage, photographed at Tinian Island prior to deployment. *(US Department of Defense)*

LEFT A total of around 120 "Fat Man" weapons were manufactured between 1947 and 1949, and the bomb was declared obsolete by 1950. A number of US museums exhibit replicas, including the National Museum of the USAF at Dayton, Ohio, and the National Museum of Nuclear Science & History, Albuquerque. *(US Department of Defense)*

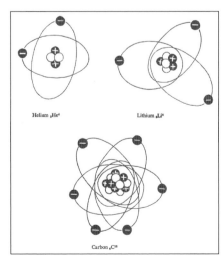

Helium ₂He⁴          Lithium ₃Li⁶

Carbon ₆C¹²

LEFT Graphical representation of the structure of atoms. *(Warehouse Collection)*

**ABOVE Technical area at the Manhattan Project where the atomic bomb was developed. Established in 1942, the project eventually employed more than 130,000 people, and cost nearly $2 billion at 1945 prices.** (Los Alamos Scientific Laboratory)

Word of what had been done in Germany soon reached Britain, the Soviet Union and the USA. In 1940, a committee of British scientists was established to report on the present state of knowledge regarding the construction of a nuclear weapon. In September 1941, a new division of the Department of Scientific and Industrial Research was created under the code name "Tube Alloys," and work started on separating uranium isotopes. At this point, Chadwick believed that Britain was the world leader in atomic weapons research, and visiting American scientists Professors G.B. Pegram and Harold C. Urey were impressed with what had been achieved, convincing the US government to create a similar project.

The American nuclear program started in 1942 using the cover name "Development of substitute materials." Huge sums of money were allocated to what was really a search for the creation of a practical atomic weapon, and the total cost was eventually close to $2 billion.

Based at the Los Alamos National Laboratory, New Mexico, the work came to be known as the Manhattan Project. The program was directed by Major General Leslie R. Groves of the US Corps of Engineers, with theoretical physicist J. Robert Oppenheimer as the scientific director. At its height, the Manhattan Project employed more than 130,000 people, and research and production took place at over 30 sites across the USA, Britain and Canada.

**LEFT Operators at calutron control panels at the Oak Ridge Y-12 plant. Designed by Ernest O. Lawrence during the Manhattan Project, the calutron was a mass spectrometer for separating isotopes of uranium.** (American Museum of Science and Energy)

Many scientists and workers from the British project were transferred to the USA. The project was considered to be so secret that even President Truman was not briefed on the development until April 25, 1945, two weeks after succeeding Roosevelt.

There was initially some doubt as to whether sufficient uranium would be available, but, by November, weapons-grade uranium-235 was being produced at the Y-12 National Security Complex at Oak Ridge, Tennessee, whilst plutonium-239 was manufactured at Hanford, Washington. In May 1945, a quantity of German uranium was captured following the country's surrender.

Towards the end of 1942, scientists at the Metallurgical Laboratory at the University of Chicago had achieved criticality – the term used to describe a perfect balance between the rate of production and loss of neutrons – in a nuclear reactor, allowing two types of atomic bomb to be developed. The first was a relatively simple gun-type fission weapon using enriched uranium-235, as typified by "Little Boy," whilst the second was a more complex implosion-type weapon based on irradiated and transmuted plutonium. The first atomic test was carried out on July 16, 1945, in the New Mexico desert at White Sands, about 250 miles (400 km) from Los Alamos. Code-named "Trinity," the implosion-type bomb – described by the scientists as "the gadget" – produced an explosive power equivalent to about 20 kilotons of TNT.

BELOW Described as "the gadget," this plutonium-based implosion-fission device was detonated during the "Trinity" test on July 16, 1945, yielding a TNT equivalent of 20 tons (18 tonnes). This was the world's first nuclear explosion. *(US Department of Defense)*

**ABOVE** During the "Trinity" test, it was originally planned that "the gadget" would be placed inside this steel flask to contain the TNT explosion if the nuclear chain reaction failed to materialize. Nicknamed "Jumbo," the 25-foot- (7.6 m-) long flask measured 10 feet (3 m) in diameter and weighed 214 tons (217 tonnes). *(US Department of Defense)*

**ABOVE RIGHT** Increasing confidence in the weapon allowed the scientists to abandon the notion of placing "the gadget" in the steel flask and "Jumbo" was suspended from a steel tower to be exposed to the effects of the atomic blast. The tower was destroyed, but "Jumbo" survived intact. *(US Department of Defense)*

**RIGHT** Robert Oppenheimer and Leslie Groves, photographed after the "Trinity" test, beside the remains of the tower from which "Jumbo" was suspended. *(US Department of Defense)*

At the Potsdam Conference in July 1945, Truman was told of the successful "Trinity" test and, in his diary, he wrote: "We have discovered the most terrible bomb in the history of the world. It may be the fire destruction prophesied in the Euphrates Valley Era, after Noah and his fabulous Ark." It was at Potsdam that Truman first told Stalin of the work that the Allies had been doing. Despite the Soviet Union's status as the third major partner in the wartime alliance, neither the USA nor Britain trusted Stalin's intentions so he had previously supposedly been kept in the dark; since he had spies deep in the Manhattan Project, however, he was perfectly aware of what was going on. Truman told Stalin that the Allies were planning to use this weapon on the Japanese to bring the war in the Pacific to an abrupt end, thus obviating the need for invasion. A plan to first mount a demonstration of the bomb which might dissuade the Japanese from continuing to fight was discounted since it would "waste" one of the only two atomic weapons that were available, so, during August 1945, bombs were dropped on the Japanese cities of Hiroshima and Nagasaki.

Although the USA remains the only nation to have deployed nuclear weapons, President Harry Truman believed that this action shortened the war and saved American lives. In August 1963, in a letter to the Chicago *Sun Times*, Truman defended his approval of the use of the bomb, claiming that it had "saved 125,000 youngsters on the American side, and 125,000 on the Japanese side from getting killed … [as well as] saving a half million youngsters on both sides from being maimed for life." But Gar Alperovitz, founder of the Democracy Collaborative, writing in his book *Atomic Diplomacy*, suggested that there was an alternative reason for the US attacks on Hiroshima and Nagasaki. Although the scale of the attacks convinced Japan that it was futile to continue with the war, the bombs also demonstrated American military might to the Soviet Union.

There is no doubt that its nuclear capability gave the USA enormous power. Brien McMahon, the US Senator for Connecticut, described the bomb as "the most important thing in history since the birth of Jesus Christ," while Arthur H. Compton, a leading US physicist and member of the Manhattan Project, even went so far as to say "atomic power is ours and who can deny that it was God's will that we should have it." While Compton may have actually believed that this was true, it soon became clear that the development of nuclear weapons was something of a double-edged sword. There was considerable popular pressure to place the weapons under the control of the newly formed United Nations (UN), and, by spring 1946, the UN Atomic Energy Commission stated that it wished to eliminate all nuclear weapons. The USA countered, presenting a plan which allowed it to control all aspects of nuclear technology – the Soviets disagreed and presented their own proposal for nuclear disarmament. Neither plan was accepted by the UN.

By July 1946, the USA had already conducted its first post-war test. Operation

**ABOVE LEFT** A nuclear explosion produces an unimaginable combination of heat, blast and light. The fireball is sufficiently intense that even the modest "Trinity" test produced a glassy residue on the desert floor, consisting of sand, quartz and feldspar that had been melted by the bomb and fused together. This residue was known as Trinitite, Atomsite or Alamogordo Glass. *(US Department of Defense)*

**ABOVE** The maximum size of the distinctive fireball, and the period of time for which it persists, depends upon the power of the weapon. This photograph was taken 16 milliseconds after the explosion of "the gadget" during the "Trinity" test; the hemisphere reaches to about 660 feet (200 m). *(US Department of Defense)*

**LEFT** In July 1946, the USA conducted atmospheric and underwater atomic tests at Bikini Atoll, code-named Operation Crossroads. The tests were assigned the names "Able" and "Baker"; the photograph shows one of the "Baker" explosions, detonated 90 feet (27 m) underwater. *(US National Archives)*

**LEFT** "Baker" test at Bikini Atoll, photographed at the moment of detonation. *(US Department of Defense)*

Crossroads saw the detonation of two weapons, code-named "Gilda" and "Helen of Bikini," at Bikini Atoll in the Pacific Ocean, designed to assess the effects of nuclear weapons on shipping. Some 95 captured Japanese vessels were anchored around the atoll and the first test saw "Gilda" detonated at a height of about 500 feet (152 m). In the second test, conducted three weeks later, "Helen" was detonated underwater at a depth of 90 feet (27 m). A third series of tests was carried out in 1948, under the name Operation Sandstone. There was no doubt that the genie was now out of the bottle – and there was to be no going back.

## Nuclear weapons in Germany

Although the USA was the first nation to successfully produce a nuclear weapon, the outcome of the Second World War would have been very different had the Nazis won the race.

In April 1939, less than six months after Hahn had reported on the discovery of nuclear fission, the Wehrmacht's Heereswaffenamt initiated a top-secret nuclear project to use fission to produce nuclear weapons. In July of that year, the Hungarian physicist Leó Szilárd is said to have warned Albert Einstein that the Germans might be working on producing an atomic bomb. Einstein, who by this time had fled Germany for the USA, signed a letter to President Franklin Roosevelt urging that the USA start work on developing its own atomic bomb.

Hitler's initial interest was in producing a "dirty bomb," or a "radiological dispersal device," that could expose Allied civilian populations to radioactive material. It was proposed that a bomb consisting of a shielded casing containing around 1,750 pounds (800 kg) of high explosive surrounded by 440 pounds (200 kg) of radioactive waste could be delivered by rocket or aircraft and would shower a large area, resulting in multiple deaths from blast, radiation sickness and genetic damage. Dropping such a device on Manhattan might have been sufficient to keep the USA out of the war in Europe.

During 1940, the Germans acquired "virtually all the uranium in Europe," totalling more than 1,200 tons (1,090 tonnes). Various experiments were planned, but the scientists seemed unable to agree on how to proceed, with rival groups working on carbon-dioxide dry ice, heavy water and electro-graphite as possible moderators for controlling the fission process. It was eventually decided that heavy water would be the most effective moderator, but it is ironic, in the light of what was to follow, that the Wehrmacht concluded that nuclear fission would have little effect in ending the war within the required timescale. In January 1942, the program was put in the hands of the Reich Research Council, and was divided among nine major institutes. Three separate projects were defined: the development of a nuclear reactor (*Uranmaschine*); the production of uranium and the separation of isotopes of uranium-235 and 238; and the production of heavy water, a project that had already been under way in Norway when the Nazis invaded. At the same time, the number of scientists working on the project was reduced. A month later, Werner Heisenberg, one of the lead scientists on the project, presented a lecture to officials of the Council describing energy acquisition from nuclear fission. Heisenberg later told Albert Speer that a bomb could not be built before 1945, and would require significant monetary and manpower resources. After the war it became apparent that he had been deliberately delaying the successful development of a German bomb. Nevertheless, at least two atomic tests were apparently carried out at the secret Nazi underground military facility in the Jonas Valley in Thuringia in 1945, with what Russian observers described as "a strong radioactive effect."

When Germany surrendered, a quantity of unprocessed uranium oxide, which was on its way to Japan by submarine, fell into the hands of the Allies.

## Nuclear weapons in Japan

In 1938, Japan had purchased a cyclotron particle accelerator from the University of California, Berkeley, and within a year Dr. Yoshio Nishina, the leading figure in the nation's atomic program, had grasped the military potential of nuclear fission. In April 1941, weapons-development programs were initiated by both the Imperial Army and the Navy, but, by 1942, the latter was convinced that an effective nuclear weapon could not be developed within a reasonable timescale. The naval program was abandoned until 1943, when it was re-established under Bunsaku Arakatsu at the Imperial University, Kyoto, and described as the F-Go Project.

Meanwhile, the Imperial Army had continued its own research, described as the Ni-Go Project. Germany was asked to collaborate, and some 1,230 pounds (560 kg) of uranium oxide was dispatched to Japan in April 1945 aboard the submarine *U-234*, along with other materials that could aid the Japanese war effort. The U-boat did not reach Japan and surrendered to the US destroyer USS *Sutton* on May 16, 1945. It is said that the fact that the submarine was carrying uranium helped convince President Truman that Japan had a nuclear program. Since there was no way of confirming progress, the USA resolved to bring the war to a swift conclusion.

## The post-war years

At the end of the Second World War, three nations had scientific programs to develop nuclear weapons. Of these, Japan and Germany were in no position to continue and the USA had already demonstrated that its technology had reached the practical stage. At least for the moment, the USA was the world's only nuclear power. It was an awesome responsibility and, around the world, many expressed their doubts as to how "the awful secret of the atomic bomb might be kept in the hands of those who are well disposed to their fellow men." As one commentator pointed out, "unlike every other instrument of aggressive war, there would seem hardly any chance of inventing an opposing weapon which would effectively counteract its destructiveness."

And yet, despite the scale of destruction that had been wrought at Hiroshima and Nagasaki, astonishingly, General MacArthur argued that nuclear weapons should be used during the Korean War. This was opposed by both President Truman and his successor, Eisenhower, at least partly on the basis that it would strengthen the Soviet view that the USA was "bent on initiating general war." As if this were not bad enough, in 1954 the USA also briefly considered using nuclear weapons to aid the French during the first Indochina War.

In November 1952, the USA detonated its first thermonuclear device. A test installation for a hydrogen, or fusion, bomb was exploded above Enewetak Atoll in the Pacific, destroying the islet Elugelab and creating a dust cloud 25 miles (40 km) high and almost 100 miles (162 km) wide. There had been conflicting views from the physicists involved as to whether work on this new weapon should go ahead, and even Robert Oppenheimer, who apparently regretted his involvement in the Manhattan Project, dragged his feet, resulting in the suspension of his security clearance. After much agonizing, the project was approved by President Truman at the end of January 1950.

Code-named "Ivy Mike," the 10.4-megaton warhead used liquid cryogenic deuterium fuel, with a fission device to initiate the fusion reaction, but the physical size of the device made it unsuitable for use as a weapon. Nevertheless, this was the first true hydrogen bomb – or "H-bomb" – using nuclear fusion for the explosive yield, rather than fission, and

**ABOVE** "Castle Bravo" was the first US test of a dry fuel hydrogen bomb; March 1, 1954, Bikini Atoll. *(US Department of Energy)*

**LEFT** The Mk 17 was the first US-designed thermonuclear device – or hydrogen bomb – to be put into mass production, with a total of 200 devices built. Weighing 21 tons (21.4 tonnes), the Mk 17 had a yield of 10 to 15 megatons. *(US Department of Defense)*

allowing the development of ever-more powerful warheads. In March 1954, during the "Bravo" trials, US scientists significantly underestimated the yield of a weapon under test. Although the projected yield was 5 megatons, the actual yield was 14.8 megatons, making it the largest weapon to be tested by the USA, and the effects of fallout were measured as far away as 300 miles (500 km) from the explosion.

While early nuclear weapons were designed to be dropped from aircraft or delivered by intercontinental ballistic missiles (ICBMs), both the USA and the Soviet Union were keen to develop smaller weapons that could be deployed against ground troops. During Operation Upshot-Knothole, a series of 11 nuclear tests conducted in May 1953, the US Army revealed the first tactical nuclear weapon in the form of the 15-kiloton W19 atomic artillery shell, designed to be fired from the M65 nuclear cannon, colloquially known as "Atomic Annie." The shell weighed 805 pounds (365 kg), and was designed to explode around 200 feet (60 m) above the target.

Tests of new weapons continued, and, during Operation Argus in 1958, a 1.7-kiloton warhead was detonated at an altitude of 125 miles (200 km), making it the first atomic weapon to be tested in space. Four years later, in May 1962 at Christmas Island, Operation Dominic 1 was the first, and only, US test of a submarine-launched ballistic missile (SLBM), using a warhead with a 600-kiloton yield.

## The Soviet Union

In 1944, Niels Bohr, a Danish physicist, had argued that the Soviet Union should be allowed to participate in the development of nuclear weapons, the better to prepare "an international control scheme" to prevent the post-war proliferation of such devices. Bohr was unsuccessful, but the Soviet Union, unhappy with its isolation and with the hostile attitude of its former allies, was only too aware of how the balance of power had shifted. Aided by spies placed strategically within the Manhattan Project, Stalin resolved that the Soviet Union should acquire its own bomb.

Yuli Khariton is considered to be the designer of the Soviet bomb, but he was helped considerably by Klaus Fuchs, a German scientist who gave the Soviets stolen plans, including details of "Fat Man," the weapon that had been used at Nagasaki. Despite difficulties in finding a supply of uranium, the first Soviet test, RDS-1, code-named "First Lightning," took place on August 29, 1949, with a weapon designated "Joe-1" by the Americans, that was almost a copy of "Fat Man." It would be fair to say that the USA was rattled, and a top-secret report, prepared by the CIA and dated June 9, 1950, concluded that "the Soviet possession of nuclear weapons has increased the military and subversive capabilities of the Soviet Union and the possibility of war … accordingly, the security of the United States is in increasing jeopardy." Appearing to support this view, it seems that, had the Soviet-backed attack in Korea in 1950

**RIGHT** "Atomic Annie" was the nickname given to the M65 atomic cannon, a 280 mm towed artillery piece capable of firing a 15-kiloton nuclear shell across a range of 20 miles (32 km). Some 200 examples were constructed, and the cannon was transported by two specially designed Kenworth tractors. *(US Department of Defense)*

been successful, Stalin might have deployed nuclear weapons against Europe.

In 1951, the Soviets conducted their second and third tests. RDS-2, code-named "Joe-2" by the Americans, was a 38.3-kiloton implosion device using tritium-boosted uranium, whilst RDS-3 ("Joe-3") was an air-dropped 41.2-kiloton weapon of composite construction, using a plutonium core and a shell of uranium. By August 1953, the Soviets had tested their first hydrogen bomb (RDS-6, or "Joe-4"), in Kazakhstan. It was a 200- to 400-kiloton thermonuclear device using layered fission and fusion fuels (uranium-235 and lithium-6 deuteride), with a fifth of the yield provided by the fusion process. "Joe-4" created something of a stir as, unlike the USA's first fusion device, it was sufficiently small to be delivered by air.

Two years later, the Soviet leader, Nikita Khrushchev, resolved that he would demonstrate his country's technology to the West by detonating a 100-megaton bomb. Dubbed "Tsar Bomba," the device was exploded in October 1961 at a height of 11,300 feet (3,700 m) above the Novaya Zemlya test site. In the event, the yield was just 58 megatons, but the heat radiation produced was enough to cause third-degree burns at a distance of 60 miles (100 km), and the yield was greater than the total explosives detonated during the Second World War. Too large to be carried inside the Soviet bombers of the period, the device was attached beneath the fuselage and special precautions were taken to prevent damage to the aircraft, with the pilot and co-pilot crew protected, inadequately as it turned out, by 600 mm of lead shielding. This was the largest nuclear device that the world had yet seen – equivalent to 1 ton (0.9 tonnes) of TNT for every head of population in Britain.

## Other nations join the "nuclear club"

Britain was frozen out of the US nuclear program in 1945, but the British government deemed it essential that the nation had independent nuclear weapons in order to remain a world power. A development program for an "independent deterrent" was initiated in January 1947, and by October 1952 Operation Hurricane saw the first bomb, with a yield

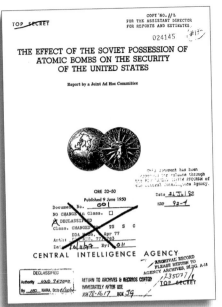

**LEFT** Secret report, prepared by the CIA in June 1950, which concluded that "the Soviet possession of nuclear weapons has increased the military and subversive capabilities of the Soviet Union and the possibility of war."
*(US National Archives)*

of 25 kilotons, tested on the Monte Bello Islands, off the coast of Australia. The first successful British hydrogen bomb, yielding 1.8 megatons, was tested in November 1957 at Christmas Island. In a fit of patriotic fervor the *Daily Express* declared: "It's our H-bomb," while those who were nervous of this new development may have taken comfort in the words of an unnamed Anglican bishop who went on record with his belief that "our nuclear weapons will be used with wisdom."

By the following year, the US political

**BELOW** Scientists Frank H. Pavry and George R. Stanbury at Monte Bello, measuring the effects of Britain's first nuclear weapon test during Operation Hurricane; October 1952.
*(Warehouse Collection)*

climate once again permitted co-operation with other nations on nuclear issues, and, in 1960, Britain's independent "Blue Streak" missile program was cancelled in favor of joint Anglo-US development. Since that date, despite using home-grown warheads, Britain has relied on the USA for a nuclear delivery system.

In February 1960, France detonated a 70-kiloton atomic weapon, code-named "Gerboise Bleu," in the Sahara Desert. Further testing was conducted underground until 1967 when a 2.6-megaton thermonuclear weapon was detonated above Fangataufa Atoll, 150 miles (240 km) south-west of the Polynesian Gambier Islands. The atoll was so contaminated with fallout that it was uninhabitable for six years, and, as late as 2006, France was still being urged to clean up the resulting radioactive mess. France conducted a further 193 nuclear tests on the Fangataufa and nearby Mururoa Atolls between 1966 and 1996. Of these, 41 were atmospheric and 137 underground; a further 15 were described as "safety trials."

China became the fifth nuclear power when it detonated a 25-kiloton uranium device in October 1964 at Lop Nur, with a hydrogen bomb successfully tested in June 1967. The Chinese weapons program was supported by the Soviet Union until the late 1950s, in exchange for a supply of uranium ore, but work continued independently after tensions emerged between the two nations.

Alongside the USA, Britain, France, the Soviet Union and China, the current roll-call of nuclear nations also includes India, Pakistan and North Korea. India and Pakistan have never agreed to be bound by the 1968 Treaty on the Non-Proliferation of Nuclear Weapons, whilst North Korea acceded from the Treaty in 1985. Israel is also usually included in the list, although it has always refused to confirm that it possesses nuclear weapons despite having been supplied with 20 tons (18 tonnes) of heavy water which the UK Atomic Energy Authority (UKAEA) had purchased from Norway in 1958. Some 150 to 200 US nuclear weapons have also been stored and deployed in Belgium, Italy, the Netherlands, Turkey and West Germany under the aegis of NATO. Similarly, former-Soviet weapons were deployed to Belarus, Kazakhstan and Ukraine following the break-up of the Soviet Union.

Other nations, including Australia, Canada, Japan and Sweden, are described as either "virtual nuclear states," or "para-nuclear states," meaning they have the technical capability to build nuclear weapons but have chosen not to do so. South Africa should also be included in this category since it not only has the capability to produce nuclear weapons, but has actually done so in the past and subsequently destroyed them.

**RIGHT** Yielding 10.4 megatons, "Ivy Mike" was the code name of the first US test of a full-scale Teller–Ulam-designed thermonuclear device. The test took place at Enewetak Atoll in the Pacific Ocean in November 1952. *(US Department of Defense)*

# East–West arms race

**D**evelopment of ever-more powerful weapons continued apace during the decades following the end of the Second World War, with huge amounts of money devoted to improving the "quality" of the weapons and increasing the number of warheads available. By 1953, both sides had developed the infinitely more powerful thermonuclear hydrogen bomb – the "H-bomb" – which used an initial fission reaction to ignite hydrogen fusion. Described as the Teller–Ulam configuration, from the names of its two chief contributors, Edward Teller and Stanislaw Ulam, the hydrogen bomb is the most efficient design for weapons, with yields above 50 kilotons. Virtually all current nuclear weapons are of the thermonuclear design.

In October 1960, President John F. Kennedy had said that: "I think the fate not only of our own civilization, but the fate of the world and the future of the human race, is involved in preventing a nuclear war." He was right but, despite a popular slogan of the period that decreed "what this planet needs is more mistletoe and less missile-talk," it didn't seem to bring an end to the madness.

From about 1957, the US Gaither Committee had used the public perception of a "missile gap" as a political tool to increase military spending, and, within a year, the US defense budget stood at $12 billion. Between 1946 and 1957, the USA amassed more than 5,000 strategic warheads with a combined payload of 5,600 megatons, a figure which the Soviet Union did not reach until the mid-1970s. By 1982, the USA had 11,000 warheads, and, by the end of the decade, was committing 7% of gross domestic product (GDP) to military expenditure. Total US defense spending during the Cold War has been estimated at about $9 trillion in present-day terms, half of which was spent on delivery mechanisms.

For a while, the Soviet Union lagged behind but, by 1986, it was reckoned to have 45,000 warheads, of which 20,000 were tactical. By this time, Soviet defense spending had risen to a crippling 15–17% of GDP, and in 1988, Soviet military spending totalled 21 billion roubles, or about $33 billion.

By the mid-1960s, the world nuclear stockpile stood at the equivalent of around 20 tons (18 tonnes) of TNT per head of population.

Following the 1962 Cuban Missile Crisis, a "hotline" was established between the Pentagon and the Kremlin, speeding communication between the two sides and reducing the possibility of misunderstandings. The hotline proved invaluable when, in November 1983, Operation Able Archer, a US-led NATO exercise involving 40,000 troops across Europe, was apparently considered to be so realistic the Soviet Union believed that a nuclear strike on its territory was a real possibility. Submarines were deployed under the Arctic ice and more than a dozen bombers put into the air with a nuclear payload.

Like gunslingers in a bad Western movie, the two sides continued to glare at one another across the plains of Germany, neither wanting to draw first but each watching the other like a hawk. Considerable sums were spent on clandestine intelligence gathering, a process that actually helped to maintain the status quo, and the world settled into what could be described as an uneasy stalemate punctuated by periods of heightened tension.

# Nuclear-weapons-free zones

**I**n an effort to prevent the spread of nuclear weapons, Article VII of the Treaty on the Non-Proliferation of Nuclear Weapons of 1970, grants nation states the right to establish specified nuclear-weapons-free zones (NWFZ). In 1975, the UN General Assembly reaffirmed that right in resolution 3472B. Nations which participate in an NWFZ have committed not to manufacture, acquire, test or possess nuclear weapons.

Although only one such treaty predates the end of the Cold War – the 1967 Treaty of Tlatelolco, which covers Latin America – there are currently nine treaties in place, establishing NWFZs that cover more than half of the earth's land area, including the South Pacific (Treaty of Rarotonga, 1985), South-East Asia (Treaty of Bangkok, 1985), Africa (Treaty of Pelindaba, 1996) and Central Asia (Treaty of Semipalatinsk, 2006), as well as the seabed, the Antarctic and space.

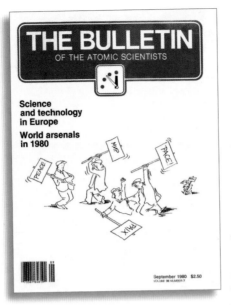

Chicago Atomic Scientists, explained that the
closer the hands came to midnight, the closer
the world was to a nuclear catastrophe. At the
time of its inception, the clock was set at seven
minutes to midnight, and, since that time, the
"hand" of the clock has moved many times, the
closest to midnight being two minutes: this first
happened in early 1953 when the USA tested
its first hydrogen bomb. The clock returned to
two minutes to midnight in 2018.

Since its inception, the concept of the clock
has subsequently been expanded to include the
effects of climate change.

# Fighting a nuclear war

In 1954, Marshal Vasily Sokolovskii, the
Soviet Chief of the General Staff, stated
unequivocally that "Soviet Forces are preparing
for combat in the atomic age," and it was
abundantly clear that the two most powerful
nations in the world, together with their
respective allies, possessed sufficient firepower
to literally wipe out life on earth. Notwithstanding
the fact that a 1957 British government White
Paper stated that "there is no defence against
nuclear war" – a view that was reinforced by
former US President Reagan's declaration that
"nuclear war cannot be won and must not be
fought" – it seems that military strategists on
both sides were not deterred from planning for
such an event.

Many strategists took the view that, although
immensely powerful, nuclear weapons were
simply another part of the legitimate arsenal
to be deployed as and when the situation
demanded. The fact that just one bomb
might be able to wipe out an entire city was a
measure of "efficiency," not a quantum change
in the logistics of conflict. Others, including
General Henry "Hap" Arnold, Commander of

## Nuclear-free zones

During the early 1980s, around 200 local
authorities in Britain, including the Greater London
Council, declared themselves to be "nuclear free,"
refusing to participate in civil defense exercises
relating to nuclear war and "forbidding" the
movement of nuclear materials through the area
controlled by the authority, although, in practice,
this was little more than a gesture.

## Doomsday clock

In 1947, a group of international researchers,
including personnel from the Manhattan
Project, developed the Doomsday Clock, a
hypothetical timepiece reflecting changes in the
level of nuclear peril facing mankind. Describing
this clock in the *Bulletin of the Atomic
Scientists*, the group, which called itself the

US Army Air Forces, took the view that nuclear weapons represented a real revolution in the technology of conflict – as had the use of bows and arrows and the invention of gunpowder. Arnold believed that nuclear weapons had "lowered the cost of destruction," making it "cheap and easy."

Nuclear weapons are frequently described in terms of being a deterrent, but what one side regards as a deterrent the other side may well view as a threat, and brinkmanship seemed to be the order of the day. For example, in 1956, speaking from the relative comfort of having a very large nuclear stockpile, US Secretary of State John Foster Dulles explained that "the ability to get to the verge without getting into the war is the necessary art … if you are scared to go to the brink you are lost." Edging to the brink of war is one thing – actually being the first to use nuclear weapons is quite another.

In 1980, the US Office of Technology Assessment estimated that a full-scale nuclear exchange would affect somewhere between 3.5 and 25 million in the USA, 16 to 44 million in the Soviet Union and 11 to 37 million elsewhere. The discrepancy between the high and low estimates is huge, but since the Hiroshima and Nagasaki attacks only involved single weapons of relatively low yield, there was little precedent for assessing the effects of larger weapons. The

numbers of casualties would also be affected, for example, by the availability of shelters and protective clothing and equipment, as well as by civil defense procedures dealing with the after-effects of an attack.

## Tactical vs strategic weapons

The proponents of nuclear warfare draw a distinction between the tactical, or non-strategic, weapons, which might be used in a limited nuclear exchange, and strategic weapons that are aimed at an entire nation, including military, economic and civilian targets, such as cities and factories. It is the strategic nuclear weapons that strike fear into the heart of the civilian population.

During the Cold War large numbers of the stockpiled weapons were tactical, meaning that they were designed for use on the battlefield, and were of a relatively low yield. For some years, the West considered that superiority in tactical nuclear weapons could offset an inferiority in conventional weapons. However, it became apparent that the Soviets had the capability of deploying either conventional or nuclear weapons at will, and if the decision was taken to use tactical nuclear weapons then multiple strikes would be made on NATO's means of delivering their own nuclear weapons, as well as at headquarters, rear area installations and communication centers. Notes produced for NATO forces in the mid-1970s regarding the deployment of Soviet ground forces suggested that the most likely scenario involved the use of 33 warheads in an initial strike, followed by a further 36 over a period of three days, 18 over the next three days and 13 for the final four days of a ten-day period, giving a total of 100 warheads.

As regards an exchange of strategic nuclear weapons, apart from the devastation that would be caused, this would have long-term effects on life on the planet, causing death, injury and genetic damage. Huge amounts of radioactive fallout would turn large areas into no-go zones, and many scientists believe that the amount of dust and particles released into the atmosphere would lead to a so-called "nuclear winter," or produce irreversible adverse effects on the environment and the ecological system that could last for decades, or even centuries, after the initial attack.

**BELOW The year 1977 saw the first trials of "Trident," a submarine-launched three-stage ballistic missile with a range exceeding 7,000 miles (11,340 km).** *(US Department of Defense)*

# Mutual assured destruction (MAD)

From 1953, believing that it possessed superior and more numerous nuclear firepower, the USA had adopted a strategy that was described as "massive retaliation." Had the Soviet Union attacked the USA with nuclear weapons then the response would have been disproportionate, "dissuading" the other side from such an action, and even as late as 1978, the historian Robert Conquest said that "there's nothing the Russians can do so long as we keep the level of our arms right." When the Soviet Union adopted a similar approach, the USA moved to a strategy described as "flexible response."

Eventually, the two sides reached near parity in the numbers and power of their weapons, so, in the interests of maintaining the uneasy stalemate, it was essential that neither side gained a technological advantage. However, even though both sides might have equal firepower, should one side decide to launch a comprehensive attack on the other, there remains a window of opportunity for the other side to react before being annihilated. This ability to react, even after having come under attack – a "second strike" – forms an intrinsic part of a strategy that came to be described as "mutual assured destruction" – a term which yields the ironically appropriate acronym MAD.

Both the strategy, and the acronym, came from the American scientist John von Neumann who was chairman of the International Ballistic Missile Committee. MAD ensured that any nation that had come under attack would be able to respond with a nuclear retaliation of at least equal force. The "balance of power," and the prospect of mutual annihilation, were key in preventing "the other side" (whichever side that was) from taking pre-emptive action: Why would any nation launch a war which neither side had any chance of winning?

There came an alarming wobble in this balance when, in March 1983, President Reagan announced the so-called "Star Wars" program. Officially described as the "strategic defense initiative" (SDI), the system would destroy incoming missiles using lasers or particle beams fired from space. If it worked, and few scientists were convinced that it would, the Soviet deterrent would have been rendered impotent. SDI may not have shaped up in the way that was originally envisaged, but the USA certainly poured large sums of money into sophisticated anti-missile defense systems. It has been suggested that the USA might, today, be able to launch a successful nuclear strike on an enemy in such a way that the opposing nuclear weapons could be eliminated before they were fired, but this seems unlikely.

# The strategy of nuclear war

D isregarding the question of who might possibly benefit from all-out nuclear war, politicians and strategists on both sides, as well as the media, have speculated endlessly on how a nuclear conflict might unfold. As early as 1946, Sir Henry Tizard had said that the use of atomic (and biological) weapons might "achieve decisive results against the civil population of a nation without a clash between the major military forces," going on to say that "some five or ten atomic bombs landed on target might well cause the evacuation of cities to an extent sufficiently seriously to sap the power of waging war by conventional means." In other words, civilians had become the primary combatants in any future major conflict.

On the other side, the situation was less clear, and, writing in the *Red Star* in August 1954, a Soviet military commentator stated that "the appearance of atomic weapons does not alter the basic principles of the organisation and conduct of the offensive battle."

The idea of a restricted nuclear strike is unlikely as, in almost any situation, the enemy would seek to destroy the nuclear weapons of opposing forces – the "use it or lose it" scenario. In practice, once the decision has been taken to use nuclear weapons, escalation would be swift and devastating. Possible scenarios that could lead to nuclear war include a deliberate aggressive act, in other words, a pre-emptive strike that leads to retaliatory action, or accident or misunderstanding.

NATO has consistently rejected demands to adopt a "no-first-use of nuclear weapons" policy – reputedly known amongst NATO officials as NOFUN – but, according to its charter, can only react to aggression from the other side. As one of the prime movers behind NATO, the USA has also refused to adopt a "no-first-use" policy, stating that "it reserves the right to use" nuclear weapons first in the case of conflict. An unofficial, if historic, British view came from Field Marshal Montgomery, who is on record as having said: "if we are attacked, we use nuclear weapons in our defence … the only proviso is that the politicians have to be asked first …

RIGHT The Soviet
Scud B (9P-117M),
seen here on its
MAZ-543 transporter-
erector-launch (TEL)
vehicle, is a tactical
missile that can be
nuclear-armed, using
warheads with a
yield of 5–80 kilotons.
(Warehouse Collection)

BELOW Making its
first appearance in
December 1997, the
Soviet "Topol-M"
(RT-2PM2) is an ICBM
mounting a single
800-kiloton warhead.
The missile is carried
on an MZKT 79221
TEL vehicle.
(Vitaly V. Kuzmin)

personally I would use the weapons first and ask afterwards."

The endless plotting of possible Soviet attacks continued through three decades, as did the military and civil defense exercises, the latter often describing obliterated cities and roving mobs of injured and starving refugees escaping from the outer fringes of the attack areas. In 1957, for example, Exercise Dutch Treat postulated that the Soviets would drop high-yield (megaton) weapons on a dozen

British and Irish cities. Two years later, a circular issued by the Ministry of Health suggested that 11 warheads, totalling 55 megatons, might be dropped in a retaliatory strike on 15 to 18 British cities. Other possible scenarios explored by the government included three 10-megaton weapons dropped on London, with single, smaller bombs dropped on other towns and cities, including Aldershot, Birmingham and Oxford. In 1962, Operation Fallex suggested that, following a sustained Soviet attack, heavily populated areas would simply be abandoned, while the casualty toll would reach 15 million.

In 1978, General Sir John Hackett (and others) published a work of fiction entitled *The Third World War*. The book was written as though in the aftermath of the world's first nuclear war, suggesting that such a conflict might have started using conventional weapons, but that, as the fighting inevitably ground to a halt, the Soviet Union would use strategic nuclear weapons to break the stalemate. The chosen target was the city of Birmingham, with a 3.4-megaton SS-17 "Spanker" missile detonated 11,500 feet (3,500 m) above the city, immediately killing 300,000, with a further 250,000 dying in the following weeks. The center of Birmingham was effectively destroyed, and surrounding areas rendered virtually impassable. In retaliation, US and British missiles were launched from submarines, targeted at the city of Minsk, wiping it out. By this time both sides had realized that further escalation would simply result in nuclear suicide and World War Three ended with the fictional collapse of the Warsaw Pact in August 1985.

Four years after the publication of Hackett's fictional scenario, the Home Office planned for the fourth, and largest, rehearsal for World War Three. Code-named Operation Hard Rock, the exercise assumed that hostilities between NATO and the Soviet Union had started on September 27, 1982, and that, within little more than a week, large areas of Britain had been reduced to a radioactive wasteland, with the politicians, military planners and local authority officers taking to their bunkers. As with Hackett's nightmare vision, the conflict started with conventional weapons, including aerial bombardment, but within days the Soviets had launched a nuclear strike that included a six-hour attack by intercontinental missiles. It was believed that an attack involving just 40 warheads would incapacitate Britain's military capability, and that less than 15% of the total Soviet nuclear arsenal would cause almost total loss of human life in Britain, destroying the nation completely. The exercise never happened because many of the local authorities who were to be involved simply refused to participate, often as part of a "nuclear-free zone" policy.

If the prospect of nuclear war by intent is distressing enough, there is an almost comic element to the notion that such an event could occur through a misunderstanding or accident. For example, back in 1980, a computer malfunction at the North American Aerospace Defense Command (NORAD) headquarters buried deep inside Cheyenne Mountain, Colorado, mistakenly informed operators that the Soviet Union had fired missiles at Washington – and the RAF was scrambled to refuel the American B-52 bombers that were sent to retaliate.

Three years later, on September 25, 1983, the Soviet *Oko* satellite-based early warning system indicated that the USA had launched a pre-emptive strike, consisting of an unlikely five missiles. Stanislav Yevgrafovich Petrov, the duty officer at the time, chose to ignore the warning, chalking it up to "computer error," and, whilst he was praised for preventing the outbreak of the Third World War, he was also reprimanded for "improper filing of paperwork."

Even after the Cold War was over, the dangers remained very real. When the USA announced in 2006 that it planned to develop a conventional warhead for the "Trident" system, the Russian President pointed out that, due to the difficulties of identifying which form of "Trident" had been deployed, "the launch of such a missile could provoke a full-scale counterattack using strategic nuclear forces." Perhaps the Americans should have painted them pink!

**LEFT** Introduced in 1954, and still flying today in a number of roles, the Boeing B-52 Stratofortress long-range bomber is probably the most iconic Cold War aircraft. It is capable of carrying both nuclear and conventional weapons, including air-launched cruise missiles. *(US Department of Defense)*

*"If the next world war is fought with nuclear weapons, the war after that will be fought with bows and arrows."*
**Albert Einstein, 1879–1955**

## Chapter Two

# Nuclear weapons

The science behind both nuclear weapons and nuclear reactors depends on exploiting the colossal amounts of energy stored in the atomic structure of the universe. This energy is released in two ways – either fission, the splitting of a heavy atom, or by fusion, the joining of light atoms. In the case of a nuclear reactor, the energy is released under careful control, but in the case of an atomic weapon it comes as an unimaginable, uncontrolled wave of heat, blast and light that dwarfs the effects of any conventional weapon. As one commentator has described it: "a million, billion, billion atoms explode in ten seconds."

OPPOSITE The world's first thermonuclear explosion – or hydrogen bomb – conducted by the USA at Enewetak Proving Grounds; November 1, 1952. *(US Department of Defense)*

All atoms consist of subatomic particles (electrons, protons and neutrons) bound together by nuclear forces, and the diameter of an individual atom is tiny, ranging from about 0.001 to 0.005 μm (0.1–0.5 nm) depending on the element involved. The positively charged protons, and neutrons, which carry no charge, form the nucleus of the atom, with negatively charged electrons circulating around the nucleus in "shells." A neutrally charged atom has an equal number of protons and electrons, and the atomic number of an element indicates the number of protons; for example, hydrogen, which is the lightest atom, has just one proton in its core and has the atomic number 1. Atoms of the same element also exist with different numbers of neutrons, and each of these variations, which are called isotopes, has an atomic mass number, expressed, for example, as uranium-235, which is equal to the number of neutrons and protons in its core. Isotopes are often unstable, and radioactive isotopes, which emit neutrons naturally, possess properties that can be exploited to release nuclear energy.

Early experiments probing the structure of the nucleus involved bombarding radioactive elements – those elements which are inherently unstable as a result of spontaneous nuclear decay – with subatomic particles. Scientists observed that some of these particles were absorbed, some "bounced" back and others passed through, with neutrons able to penetrate all materials. German chemists Hahn and Strassmann noticed that, while bombarding uranium atoms with neutrons, the nucleus would sometimes fission, at the same time releasing additional neutrons and large amounts of energy. The neutrons that were released had the same effect as those that had been used to bombard the nucleus, with yet more energy and more neutrons being released, leading to what was described as a "chain reaction." Some of the neutrons released escape from the fissionable material and, if neutrons are lost at a faster rate than they are produced, the chain reaction will not be self-sustaining. In order to be successful, a nuclear reaction must effectively control the loss of neutrons, and the point at which the neutrons being lost are matched by those being produced is described as the "critical mass." A nuclear explosion can only occur if there is sufficient fissionable material to exceed the critical mass.

At first it was believed that the phenomenon could only be created using either uranium-235, which was thought to be extremely rare, or the man-made element plutonium, which had been produced in 1940 by bombarding uranium-238 with deuterons – stable particles consisting of a proton and a neutron. Introducing a neutron into just one uranium-235 nucleus causes it to divide into two lighter and simpler elements, for example barium-141 and krypton-92, described as the fission products. The sum of the atomic weights (ie the total number of protons and neutrons combined) of the fission products is always less than the atomic weight of the original atom because some of the mass is released as free neutrons, yielding millions of electron-volts of energy. The use of sufficient

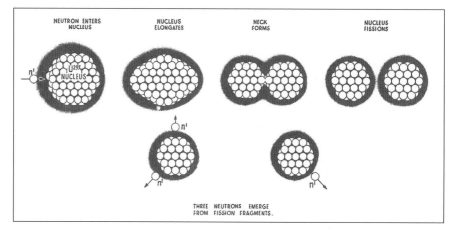

**RIGHT Mechanics of fission in uranium-235.**
*(Warehouse Collection)*

quantities of uranium – or plutonium – results in a chain reaction that can be used to create a bomb of colossal power, and even a modest atomic bomb has the explosive power of thousands of tons of conventional explosive.

The first atomic bomb, "Little Boy," used two slugs of compressed uranium-235 assembled into either end of a "gun barrel"; an explosive charge at one end fired one of these slugs of fissionable material down the barrel, where it combined with the other to form a critical mass. This was the technology used in the bomb detonated above the city of Hiroshima, and, although it was extremely inefficient, with only an estimated 1.7% of its material fissioning, the weapon yielded a blast equivalent of 15,000 tons (13,600 tonnes) of TNT from less than 2.2 pounds (<1 kg) of uranium. A further 25 "Little Boy" bombs were constructed in 1947, but all had been withdrawn from service by 1951.

The "gun" technique used for "Little Boy" was not feasible with plutonium but the material was unstable enough that a chain reaction could be initiated spontaneously without the slugs of fissionable material reaching maximum compression. "Fat Man" used an "implosion" technique by surrounding a ball of a little more than 2.2 pounds (>1 kg) of plutonium with conventional high explosive. When the explosive was detonated, a wave of pressure created a chain reaction in the plutonium, resulting in a blast of destructive energy equal to about 21,000 tons (19,000 tons) of TNT. Another 120 "Fat Man" bombs were manufactured between 1947 and 1949, but the design was considered obsolete by 1950. These early weapons were primitive by modern standards, producing modest yields. Further research was directed at reducing the physical size of the bomb, as well as improving the yield and reliability.

A breakthrough occurred with Edward Teller's development of the thermonuclear bomb, a device that increases the potential yield a thousandfold, from kilotons to megatons. Thermonuclear weapons are based on nuclear fusion, a process that creates new elements by fusing light ones together using a mixture of extreme pressure and heat to overcome the natural electrostatic repulsion that exists between the positive charges of atomic nuclei. The process results in a loss of atomic mass

LEFT **Billet of highly enriched uranium, in which the uranium-235 content has been increased by isotope separation. Uranium is a silvery-white naturally radioactive heavy metallic element in the actinide series of the periodic table.** *(Ames Laboratory; US Department of Energy)*

ABOVE **Schematic diagram of a gun-type fission weapon; this technology was adopted for "Little Boy," the bomb dropped on Hiroshima.** *(Warehouse Collection)*

BELOW **Schematic diagram of implosion-type fission weapon. This technology was adopted for "Fat Man," the bomb used at Nagasaki.** *(Warehouse Collection)*

FAR RIGHT Edward
Teller was one of
those involved in the
Manhattan Project,
leaving at the end
of the war. In 1950,
he returned to Los
Alamos and, with
Stanislaw Ulam,
started work on a
thermonuclear fusion
weapon. The first US
thermonuclear weapon
was detonated in
November 1952. *(US
Department of Energy)*

which produces a huge amount of fusion energy. The first tentative thermonuclear bomb, detonated by the Americans in 1951, was effectively a hybrid device, with an atomic primary stage to initiate the secondary, thermonuclear, fusion stage, using isotopes of hydrogen such as deuterium or tritium which were fused to produce helium. The temperatures involved in the process are in the order of 60 million degrees Kelvin, and the amount of energy released depends entirely on the amount of material present in the reaction.

A year later, the first full-scale thermonuclear weapon, code-named "Ivy Mike," with a yield of 10.4 megatons, was detonated on Enewetak Atoll. A large fission bomb was used to trigger the reaction, with liquid deuterium as the fusion fuel. Cryogenic equipment was required to maintain the deuterium in a liquid state, and, although the blast was equivalent to several megatons of TNT, and the heat wave was felt 30 miles (50 km) away, this could scarcely be considered a viable weapon. Subsequent devices employed a solid sheath of lithium deuteride, and later weapons employed a three-stage process, described as fission-fusion-fission, using a fission bomb to detonate a fusion reaction in lithium-deuteride, sufficient to produce fission in a mass of uranium. This gives a relatively compact weapon producing large quantities of fission products, with the potential for releasing unlimited energy.

Although factually incorrect, this type of weapon is generally described as a "hydrogen bomb" or "H-bomb" – a term that has become firmly lodged in the public imagination.

## Other types of atomic bomb

In February 1950, the Hungarian-American physicist Leó Szilárd, who had conceived the use of a nuclear chain reaction as a weapon, described a possible "cobalt bomb" consisting of either a fission or fusion weapon with a sheath of metallic cobalt or a similar material. Its use would result in radiation poisoning that would be sufficient to render affected areas uninhabitable for a century or more. Cobalt weapons were seriously investigated by the USA, but none were ever built or deployed.

The USA, the Soviet Union, France and China have also developed "neutron bombs" or "enhanced-radiation weapons." A low-yield thermonuclear device is constructed in such a way that, rather than being absorbed, the neutrons generated by the fusion reaction are intentionally allowed to escape through a thin casing. A neutron bomb emits about ten times the amount of neutron radiation as a conventional fusion weapon, and is designed specifically to kill by the use of radiation, with a minimal effect on infrastructure through blast or heat.

## Development and testing

To ensure that a nuclear device will function correctly, and to assess its likely effect when used, it is necessary to conduct test detonations, and, although a test might be able to demonstrate how a specific weapon performs, it cannot indicate the effect of simultaneously detonating multiple weapons over a relatively small area.

ABOVE Operation Upshot-Knothole was a series of nuclear tests carried out in 1953 at the Nevada Test Site. The largest device of the series was "Ruth," with a yield of 200 kilotons; the smallest was "Dixie," yielding just 11 kilotons. *(US National Nuclear Security Administration, Nevada Field Office)*

Early nuclear tests were made by detonating the device on a tower or suspended from a balloon, or by dropping it from an aircraft. The first underground test was conducted in 1951, and the majority of the tests carried out during the Cold War were underground. This has the advantage that the explosion is contained, and, providing there is no "venting" to the surface, fallout is minimized.

The warhead, or "physics package" as it is often termed, is generally tested without the delivery vehicle, and the USA, for example, has conducted fewer than ten tests using an operational missile. Most notable of these was a single test of an ICBM with a nuclear payload during Operation Frigate Bird, when a "Polaris A2" missile was launched from a submarine across a distance of more than 1,000 miles (1,600 km) to a test site on Christmas Island.

Testing also has a propaganda value. Successful nuclear tests have been used to

RIGHT "Minuteman" ICBM, capable of carrying up to three nuclear warheads, with a yield of 300–500 kilotons. "Minuteman" is currently the only ICBM in the US nuclear arsenal. *(US Department of Defense)*

signal the scientific and military strength of the
particular nation and, between 1945 and 1963,
the world's nuclear powers conducted almost
600 tests in the atmosphere, with a total yield
of 545 megatons. Concerns began to arise
that the biosphere was being contaminated
by radioactivity: scientific monitoring systems
showed that testing was having a measurable
effect on levels of environmental radioactive
particles and particular concerns were raised
about the levels of radioactive isotopes (or
radionuclides). Levels of strontium-90 in milk
rose considerably following periods of intense

testing during 1961 and 1962, and there were
measurable increases in tritium (hydrogen-3)
and caesium-137, all of which have biological
effects, including damage to DNA and an
increase in various cancers. Discussions about
limiting testing, involving the USA, Britain, the
Soviet Union, Canada and France, had started
back in 1955, but it was not until August 1963
that the Treaty Banning Nuclear Weapon Tests
in the Atmosphere, in Outer Space and Under
Water was signed.

The Treaty did not result in an end to all
testing, and, since 1963, a further 1,352 tests
have been conducted underground with a
total yield of 90 megatons. However, there
was a measurable reduction in environmental
concentrations of specific radionuclides. In
1976, the USA and the Soviet Union agreed
to limit the yield of underground tests to
a maximum of 150 kilotons. Underground
testing continued in the USA until 1992, in the
Soviet Union until 1990 and in Britain to 1991.
China and France ended testing in 1996, but,
in January 2016, North Korea, which had
started testing in October 2006, claimed that
it had successfully tested a "miniaturized"
thermonuclear device.

## Nuclear test sites

The tests for the first atomic weapons were
carried out at White Sands Proving Ground near
Alamogordo, New Mexico, but, by the 1950s,
the USA had established a test site in Nye
County, Nevada, with the first test conducted
there on January 27, 1951. Mushroom clouds
rising above the site were visible for hundreds
of miles and radioactive fallout was often carried
by the wind across the state of Utah, leading
to a rise in some forms of cancer, including
leukemia. Various schemes are currently in
operation to compensate those living downwind
of the Nevada Test Site who may have been
affected; by 2006, the compensation figure paid
to US citizens exposed to nuclear hazards as a
result of the nuclear weapons program stood at
$1.2 billion.

The USA also tested weapons at a
number of sites in the Pacific, including the
Marshall Islands, from 1946 until about 1960,
the first being Bikini Atoll. More than 100
atmospheric tests were carried out until the

**RIGHT** Shell of a typical domestic house constructed at the Nevada Test Site to observe the effects of nuclear weapons on small-scale structures; 1955. *(US National Archives)*

**BELOW** Crater resulting from a shallow underground 104-kiloton blast carried out during Operation Plowshare at the Yucca Flat Test Site in July 1962; the crater measured 1,280 feet (390 m) in diameter and was 320 feet (97 m) deep. The blast was part of a program designed to investigate the use of nuclear weapons for mining and other civilian purposes. *(US Department of Defense)*

**LEFT** Multiple craters resulting from nuclear blasts at the Yucca Flat Test Site. *(US Department of Defense)*

**LEFT** Explosives storage area at the Foulness Test Site of the AWE. The site was in use for the entire period of the Cold War and was used during the development of all of Britain's nuclear weapons, as well as for conducting investigations into the effects of nuclear weapons on buildings. *(Historic England)*

ratification of the Partial Test-Ban Treaty in 1963 when testing reverted to Nevada. Many of the Pacific islands that were used for testing remain contaminated to this day, and the USA has paid more than $750 million to Marshall Islanders in compensation.

Between 1952 and 1957, a total of 12 major tests, and many minor tests, were carried out by the British at sites in Australia, including Emu Field, at Maralinga in the Great Victoria Desert in South Australia and at the Monte Bello Islands, an archipelago of around 174 small islands off the coast of north-west Australia. Further small-scale testing continued at Emu Field until 1963. Radioactivity from the mainland tests was detected in South Australia, New South Wales, the Northern Territory and Queensland. The sites at Emu Field and at the Monte Bello Islands were both seriously contaminated, with "significant radiation hazards" remaining even after a 1967 clean-up; at Maralinga, a second attempt to decontaminate the site was made in the year 2000 at a cost of $108 million. More British tests were conducted on Christmas Island in the Indian Ocean during 1957 and 1958, and at Malden Island in the Pacific. All solo British testing ended in 1958, with joint tests being conducted by Britain and the USA from 1961 at Nellis Air Force Range and the Nevada Test Site.

The health effects of the British tests were no less serious, and, in 2005, a study concluded that sailors who observed the tests at Malden Island suffered adverse effects from exposure to fallout; although subsequently unsuccessful, a class action was filed against the Ministry of Defence (MoD). The Australian government has also paid compensation to former personnel who have suffered health problems, including servicemen who were ordered to watch the tests without any proper protective equipment, and to the Aboriginal Maralinga Tjarutja people.

Soviet weapons tests, both atmospheric and underground, were generally carried out at the Southern Test Site in Semipalatinsk, north-east Kazakhstan, using the Degelen Mountain Test Facility. This was said to be the largest underground nuclear test site in the world, with 181 tunnels, and some 450 tests made here between 1949 and 1989. There was also a Northern Test Site at Novaya Zemlya, an Arctic Ocean archipelago in north Russia, where a

## TABLE 1 NUMBERS OF TESTS CONDUCTED BY THE NUCLEAR POWERS

| Nation | Number of tests | | | |
|---|---|---|---|---|
| | Atmosphere | Underground | Underwater | Total |
| **Tests conducted between July 16, 1945, and August 5, 1963:*** | | | | |
| Britain | 21 | 2 | – | 23 |
| France | 4 | 4 | – | 8 |
| Soviet Union | 212 | – | 3 | 215 |
| USA | 222 | 114 | 5 | 341 |
| **Tests conducted after August 6, 1963:** | | | | |
| Britain | – | 20 | – | 20 |
| China | 23 | 22 | – | 45 |
| France | 41 | 134 | – | 175 |
| India | – | 5 | – | 5 |
| Israel/South Africa** | 1 | – | – | 1 |
| North Korea | – | 4 | – | 4 |
| Pakistan | – | 2 | – | 2 |
| Soviet Union | – | 464 | – | 464 |
| USA | – | 598 | – | 598 |
| **Total number of tests conducted between 1945 and 2015, 1,901*** | | | | |

* The Partial Test-Ban Treaty, 1963, prohibited testing in the atmosphere and underwater.

** There are suggestions that Israel and South Africa conducted a joint test near Prince Edward Island in 1979; the incident, which is known as the South Atlantic Flash, was picked up by American instruments.

*** Accurate numbers of tests are difficult to verify; other sources suggest that the number of tests conducted since 1945 may be as high as 2,119.

further 224 tests were carried out, including the 1961 test of the 50-megaton "Tsar Bomba," the most powerful nuclear weapon detonated during the Cold War. Soviet nuclear weapons tests were also conducted in Uzbekistan, Ukraine and Turkmenistan.

The Soviet authorities showed little regard for the effects of testing on the local people or environment, and the consequences of exposure to radiation were rarely made public at the time. For example, the Novaya Zemlya site has been identified as the largest single cause of radioactive contamination in the Arctic, while testing at the Semipalatinsk site has been estimated to have impacted the health of some 200,000 local residents. The Semipalatinsk site was closed in 1991, and unguarded fissile material, including quantities of plutonium, was abandoned in tunnels and boreholes. Five years later, a team of Kazakh, Russian and American nuclear scientists and engineers, operating under the strictures of the Nunn–Lugar Cooperative Threat Reduction Program, started a six-year operation to secure these materials, filling boreholes with concrete and sealing the entrances to tunnels.

Other nuclear nations carried out tests in whatever domestic areas were sufficiently remote to maintain secrecy and to protect the population. France, at first, favored areas of the Sahara Desert in Algeria, which was a French colony until 1962, but, for tests conducted between 1966 and 1970, chose atolls in the French Polynesian Islands. Chinese nuclear tests were generally carried out at Lop Nur, a dried-out salt lake in Mongolia (see Tables 1 and 2, pages 40 and 41).

# Effects of nuclear weapons

The destructive effects of nuclear weapons are threefold, consisting of blast, heat and radiation.

A main difference between a nuclear weapon and a conventional weapon is power. For example, one of the largest pieces of conventional ordnance is the US Air Force's (USAF's) "mother of all bombs," the GBU-43/B "massive ordnance air blast," equivalent to about 11 tons (10 tonnes) of TNT. The Soviet Union claimed to have a "father of all bombs"

## TABLE 2 NUCLEAR TEST SITES

| Nation | Test site locations |
|---|---|
| Britain | Christmas Island; Emu Field, South Australia; Maralinga, South Australia; Malden Island; Monte Bello Islands |
| China | Lop Nur, Xinjiang Uygur Province |
| France | Fangataufa, Tuamotu Archipelago; Mururoa, Tuamotu Archipelago; Reggane, Algeria |
| India | Pokhran Test Range, Rajasthan |
| North Korea | Punggye-ri Nuclear Test Site, North Hamgyong Province |
| Pakistan | Ras Koh Hills, Balochistan Province |
| Soviet Union | Novaya Zemlya, north Russia; Degelen Mountain Test Facility, Semipalatinsk, Kazakhstan; also various sites in Uzbekistan, Ukraine and Turkmenistan |
| USA | Alamogordo, New Mexico; Marshall Islands; Nevada Test Site, Nye County, Nevada;  Nellis Air Force Range, Nevada |

– the so-called "aviation thermobaric bomb of increased power" – a fuel-air weapon with a blast equivalent to 44 tons (40 tonnes) of TNT, said to have a similar effect to a tactical nuclear weapon but without radioactive fallout. To put this into perspective, a nuclear explosion of 10 kilotons, a bomb with 40% less power than the 15-kiloton bomb dropped on Hiroshima, is 250 to 1,000 times more powerful than either of these weapons. Larger devices, with yields measured in megatons, can be a million times more powerful.

As with a conventional weapon, blast crushes and destroys objects in its path, but, unlike a conventional weapon, which can be considered to be like a hammer blow, the shock wave from a nuclear explosion is more of a prolonged "push": the duration of the blast continuing hundreds of times longer than a conventional high-explosive bomb. In the case of an air burst, elements of the shock wave are also reflected from the ground, which has been heated and compressed, and these elements travel faster than the direct wave, effectively catching it up and reinforcing it. There is also an extended negative or "suction" phase which has an equal potential to cause damage. The effect of the blast on personnel is considered irrelevant because, at the distances at which it would kill, the effects of the subsequent heat and radiation are much greater.

The blast is followed by a massive wave of

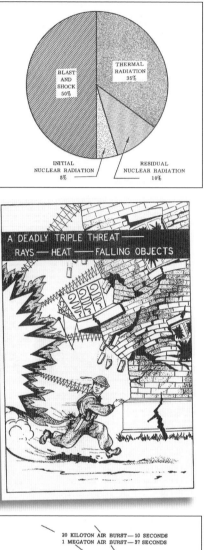

intense light and heat, and a release of radiation. The light and heat will actually arrive at the target before the slower-moving blast wave, whilst the radioactive products resulting from the disintegration of the bomb itself arrive later.

Directly beneath the explosion is the area described as "ground zero." Here, at the moment of the explosion, an intense ball of fire rises up on a column of hot gas thousands of feet into the air, carrying vaporized rock, dust, smoke and debris, whilst strong after-winds also carry debris into the air. The column billows out at the top into the distinctive mushroom shape. Most of the heat is produced within the first second of the explosion, and the temperature is dependent on the type of weapon and not its yield. An Australian Army manual written in 1955 to describe the effects of atomic weapons stated that, 0.1 milliseconds after detonation, the ball of fire consists of "an isothermal sphere with a radius of 50ft (15.25m) at a temperature of 300,000°K"; later estimates for thermonuclear weapons put the temperature at 10,000,000°K. At close range, the wave of heat and light, which includes infrared, ultraviolet light, is lethal, but even at some distance is capable of causing blindness and severe burns, as well as starting a firestorm.

The third effect of a nuclear weapon consists of radiation produced during the fission process in the form of penetrating gamma rays and neutrons, both of which are lethal. Alpha and beta particles are also produced as a result of the decay of the products of fission, and neutron-induced activity in the soil and in other materials. The initial period of radiation is brief, but transitions into a much longer period, during which there is considerable residual radiation. Some of the radiation products created exhibit a half-life – the time it takes for half the nuclei in a radioactive substance to disintegrate spontaneously – that can range from days to millennia. For example, caesium-137, which is a major source of radiation in nuclear fallout, has a half-life of 30 years, while the half-life of uranium-235 is more than 700 million years and that of uranium-238 is 4.5 billion years.

And, sadly, the notion that cockroaches will be the only creatures to survive a nuclear war is a myth. While a dose of 1,000 rads – the standard centimeter–gram–second (CGS) measurement for absorbed radiation – is sufficient to kill a human being after just ten minutes, even a cockroach cannot survive beyond 20,000 rads. Some insects can survive higher rates of exposure, but the bacteria *Deinococcus radiodurans*, which has been dubbed "Conan the Bacterium," can resist 1.5 million rads, and in a genetically modified form has been used to digest heavy metal and solvent residues during clean-up operations on highly radioactive sites.

## Electro-magnetic pulse

Nuclear explosions, particularly those occurring in the upper atmosphere, also create an electro-magnetic pulse (EMP) as the wave of gamma rays hit the upper atmosphere. This surge of electro-magnetic radiation is reflected back at the earth at the speed of light across a wide area, travelling along power lines, cables, metal surfaces, antennas and so on. A power line that is several miles long will absorb tens of thousands of amps, which will disrupt, damage or destroy sensitive electrical and electronic equipment by inducing surges of current and voltage. The pulse can affect communications systems, computing equipment and electronics used, for example, in aircraft and motor vehicles. The effect is not consistent, but a deliberate EMP attack has the capacity to totally destroy a nation's military and civilian electrical and technological infrastructure, effectively turning the clock back to the 19th century.

It is possible to make electronic components and systems resistant to this damage, and to the possibility of malfunction, by a process described as "radiation hardening."

## US nuclear weapons

The nuclear weapons deployed against Hiroshima and Nagasaki were physically large – "Little Boy," for example, was 10 feet (3 m) long and weighed 9,700 pounds (4,400 kg) – and were simply dropped from a modified Boeing B-29 Superfortress. For tactical weapons this remained the optimum situation for some years. Smaller weapons were subsequently developed, capable of being delivered by short- and medium-range rockets or fired from cannons, but the introduction of ICBMs during the 1950s was considered something of a turning point. ICBMs offered a more reliable and less vulnerable means of delivery across long distances, but, from the beginning of the 1960s, started to be replaced by submarine-launched weapons with a range of more than 3,000 miles (5,000 km).

To date, the USA has produced over 100 different types of nuclear warhead and dozens of delivery vehicles. Early weapons were identified using "mark" numbers, with the series running from Mk 4 to Mk 101, with "Little Boy," the abandoned "Thin Man" and "Fat Man" being considered Mks 1 to 3. Around 1960, this practice was discontinued, with later weapons identified by an alphanumeric "W" or "B" code: the "W" prefix, for example W78, indicates that the specific weapon is a warhead, whilst "B" identifies a bomb designed to be delivered by aircraft. Individual US nuclear weapons are described, according to their method of delivery, in Chapters Four to Six.

Although NATO currently includes three nuclear states – the USA, Britain and France – the USA continues to provide the majority of NATO's "nuclear umbrella." For logistical reasons, a large proportion of the US European nuclear stockpile was based in Britain during the Cold War, and in a pamphlet published at the beginning of the 1980s, the Campaign for Nuclear Disarmament (CND) claimed that the USA had more than 100 "military facilities" in Britain, including 17 weapons dumps. In 1981, the announcement that 160 US cruise missiles would be based at Greenham Common and Molesworth saw the beginnings of a protest that would continue for almost 20 years, and, even as late as 2005, the *Guardian* was claiming that there were still over 100 American nuclear warheads in store at RAF Lakenheath.

# Independent British nuclear deterrent

Although Britain developed an "independent nuclear deterrent," US bombs and missiles were stationed in Britain, and, for that matter, elsewhere across the world, throughout the Cold War. Britain also provided bases for US bombers and early warning equipment, and these weapons and facilities helped to provide a nuclear shield for Britain and Europe. Unfortunately, they also ensured Britain was a target for the Soviet Union.

However, the notion of Britain's "independent deterrent" is, at least partly, an illusion. In 1955, Churchill spoke of Britain possessing "the most up-to-date nuclear weapons, and the means of delivering them," but, in truth, Britain has tended to rely on US technology. Moreover, Britain's Cold War posture, including the choice of targets, was almost entirely dependent on the USA, with operational control of the V-Bomber force, and the subsequent "Polaris" and "Trident" weapons, assigned to the Supreme Allied Commander Atlantic (SACLANT).

### The British nuclear bomb

Research into the development of nuclear weapons in Britain started in 1940 when two scientists working at the University of Birmingham, Otto Frisch and Rudolf Peierls, suggested that the fission of uranium-235 could

BELOW Developed during the late 1950s, "Atlas" was one of the first ground-launched ICBMs, and was capable of delivering a 1.44-megaton W49 warhead across 9,000 miles (14,500 km). *(US Department of Defense)*

provide the basis for a weapon. A year later, a report on the military application of uranium fission was produced under the direction of Sir Henry Tizard. A copy was sent to the Uranium Committee in the USA, ultimately leading to the creation of the Manhattan Project and the subsequent bombing of Hiroshima and Nagasaki in 1945. British scientists Otto Frisch, Rudolf Peierls, Geoffrey Taylor and William Penney were among those transferred to the USA to support the project.

In 1946, the US Atomic Energy Act – often described as the McMahon Act – outlawed co-operation in research and development on nuclear weapons between the USA and other nations. With no alternative course available if Britain was also to have nuclear weapons, in 1947 Prime Minister Clement Attlee authorized the development of an independent British nuclear weapons program. The work was led by Dr. William Penney, the then Chief Superintendent of Research and Armaments, with Lord Portal appointed as Controller of Production, Atomic Energy. In June 1947, Penney began putting his research and development team together to design a plutonium bomb. The project was initially based at Woolwich Arsenal in south-east London, with contributions coming from the nearby Armaments Research and Development Establishment at Fort Halstead in Kent. Construction work on reactors for the production of plutonium started in September 1947 at Sellafield in Cumbria, with the first reactor completed by October 1950; the plutonium plant came on line in April 1952. The military research program was moved from Woolwich to a former RAF airfield at Aldermaston in Berkshire in 1950, and two years later the site became known as the Atomic Weapons Research Establishment (AWRE), operating under the auspices of the Ministry of Supply (MoS). In 1954, all British atomic research was transferred to the UKAEA, and a year later, the decision was taken to develop a British thermonuclear device.

There were also commercial aspects to the project, and work was carried out at Harwell in Oxfordshire and Risley in Lancashire to exploit nuclear fission for energy production. Britain's first nuclear reactor, known as Britain

Experimental Pile Zero, was commissioned at Risley in July 1948.

The first weapon, a plutonium implosion device with a yield of 25 kilotons, code-named "Hurricane," was ready for testing by October 1952. Clearly there was nowhere in Britain where tests could be conducted, and the device was detonated inside the hold of the obsolete frigate HMS *Plym*, anchored offshore at Trimouille Island in the Monte Bello Islands group. The ship was almost completely vaporized and the weapon created a large crater on the seabed. Before the test had been carried out, Penney had suggested that, although timing was "tight," it might be possible for a "completely-proven weapon to be in service by mid-1954."

By November 1953, "Hurricane" had evolved into "Blue Danube," sometimes described as "Smallboy" or "atom bomb Mk 1." "Blue Danube" was a 10- to 12-kiloton air-dropped free-fall bomb based on the American Mk 4. It was developed for production into a composite plutonium/uranium weapon capable of being carried in the bomb-bays of Britain's V-Bombers. A series of four tests were conducted at Emu Field, South Australia, under the code name Operation Totem, and plans were drawn up to manufacture a stockpile of up to 800 of these weapons, although, in fact, less than 60 were actually constructed. The first example was delivered to RAF Wittering

**ABOVE** The first nuclear weapon to be produced by Britain in quantity was code-named "Blue Danube," a 10- to 12-kiloton composite plutonium/uranium air-dropped free-fall bomb based on the American Mk 4. A total of about 60 examples were constructed. *(RAF Museum, Crown Copyright)*

**LEFT** Designed to be delivered by V-Bomber, "Blue Danube" was a physically large weapon. It measured 24 feet (7.32 m) in length, and the complete weapon weighed 10,000 pounds (4,636 kg). *(Warehouse Collection)*

**BELOW** In 1958, "Blue Danube" was replaced by the more compact "Red Beard"; the latter had a tritium-boosted fissile core, with a yield of 15–25 kilotons. The smaller size of this weapon allowed up to four to be carried in a V-Bomber. This example was photographed at the test compound of the **AWE.** *(RAF Museum, Crown Copyright)*

**BELOW** Dating from 1955, "Orange Herald" was a fission-fusion weapon with a yield of 720 kilotons, designed to be mounted on a missile. *(Warehouse Collection)*

in November 1953, despite no aircraft being available until the following year. "Blue Danube" was replaced by the more compact "Red Beard" in 1958, using a tritium-boosted fissile core, with a yield of 15 to 25 kilotons.

Operation Mosaic, which was also conducted at Trimouille Island, during May and June 1956, was intended to further the development of a British thermonuclear device. By January 1957, this led to the development of two alternative devices: "Green Granite," intended to be delivered by missile, and "Orange Herald." There were large and small versions of both weapons, but, at the last minute, the large version of "Green Granite" was replaced by a third device code-named "Purple Granite." During November 1957, a series of tests described as Operation Grapple showed that the performance was below expectations and it wasn't until later in the year that the yields were increased to around 1 to 3 megatons.

A number of test series were also carried out involving nuclear material used in conjunction with a conventional explosion in order to study, for example, the dispersal of radiation.

Following the successful "Grapple" tests, the first deployable British thermonuclear weapon appeared in the form of "Yellow Sun" Mk 1, using a tamper-boosted "layer cake" warhead code-named "Green Bamboo," but this was subsequently replaced by the "Green Grass" pure-fission warhead, and then by the "Red

Snow" warhead, similar to the American W28. In this latter form, the weapon was described as "Yellow Sun" Mk 2, and is often considered to be the definitive British thermonuclear weapon. The first of around 150 examples of "Yellow Sun" Mk 2 entered service in 1961, displacing the existing "Blue Danube." The "Green Grass" warhead was also installed in a modified "Blue Danube" casing, but the resulting weapon, known as "Violet Club," was fragile and unreliable and only a handful were produced.

**BELOW** Following the successful "Grapple" tests, the first deployable British thermonuclear weapon appeared in the form of "Yellow Sun" Mk 1, seen here during loading trials with a Vulcan bomber at Farnborough; 1962. *(RAF Museum, Crown Copyright)*

RIGHT "Blue Steel"
missile being loaded
into a modified
Vulcan bomber at
RAF Scampton; 1963.
"Blue Steel" was an
air-to-surface strategic
missile carrying a
1.1-megaton
"Red Snow"
thermonuclear
warhead.
*(RAF Museum, Crown
Copyright)*

## TABLE 3 BRITISH NUCLEAR BOMBS, MISSILES AND WARHEADS IN SERVICE 1953–80

| Date in service | Designation | Description | Range (where applicable) | Yield |
|---|---|---|---|---|
| **Bombs and missiles** | | | | |
| 1953 | "Blue Danube" Mk 1, Mk 2 | Free-fall bomb; composite plutonium/uranium fission warhead | – | 10–12 kilotons |
| 1958 | "Violet Club" | Free-fall bomb; "Green Grass" uranium fission warhead | – | 500 kilotons |
| 1958 | "Yellow Sun" Mk 1 | Free-fall bomb; "Green Bamboo" or "Green Grass" uranium fission warhead | – | 400 kilotons |
| 1960 | "Red Beard" | Free-fall bomb; tritium-boosted plutonium/uranium fission warhead | – | 15–25 kilotons |
| 1961 | "Yellow Sun" Mk 2 | Free-fall bomb; "Red Snow" thermonuclear fusion warhead | – | 1.1 megatons |
| 1962 | "Blue Steel" | Air-to-surface strategic stand-off missile; "Red Snow" thermonuclear fusion warhead | 120 miles (200 km) | 1.1 megatons |
| 1966 | WE177B | Free-fall bomb; thermonuclear fusion warhead | – | 450 kilotons |
| 1969 | "Ikara" | Ship-launched nuclear depth charge; WE177A thermonuclear fusion warhead | 12 miles (19 km) | 0.5 kilotons |
| 1969 | WE177A | Free-fall bomb; thermonuclear fusion warhead | – | 0.5–10 kilotons |
| 1980 | WE177C | Free-fall bomb; thermonuclear fusion warhead | – | 200 kilotons |
| **Warheads** | | | | |
| 1954 | "Green Bamboo" | Fission-fusion warhead | – | 1 megaton |
| 1954 | "Green Granite" | Fission-fusion warhead | – | 1 megaton |
| 1955 | "Orange Herald" | Fission-fusion warhead | – | 720 kilotons |
| 1957 | "Green Grass" | Fission warhead | – | 400 kilotons |
| 1958 | "Red Snow" | Thermonuclear fusion warhead | – | 1.1 megatons |
| 1970 | ET317 | Thermonuclear fission-fusion-fission warhead for British "Polaris" ballistic missiles | – | 200 kilotons |
| 1982 | "Chevaline" | Thermonuclear fission-fusion-fission multiple warhead for British "Polaris" ballistic missiles | – | 200 kilotons |

The last all-British nuclear warhead and delivery vehicle was the Avro "Blue Steel," an air-to-surface strategic missile carrying a 1.1-megaton "Red Snow" thermonuclear warhead. Described as a "stand-off" weapon, meaning that it could be launched against a target whilst the launch vehicle remained outside the range of enemy surface-to-air missiles, "Blue Steel" was designed to be carried by a Vulcan or Victor bomber. Development started in 1956, with the first of around 50 examples entering service in December 1962; the last was withdrawn at the end of 1970. A long-range version, designated "Blue Steel II," was briefly considered, but was cancelled in favor of the American "Skybolt" system.

By 1961, British research into independent delivery systems had ended and all further developments were made in co-operation with the USA.

The last tactical nuclear warhead used by the British armed forces, and the last nuclear weapon to serve with the RAF, was WE177, a warhead suitable for delivery by air as either a bomb or a helicopter-launched depth charge. The design of WE177 had been initiated in 1960 under the original designation RE179, when Britain had agreed it would purchase the American "Skybolt" system. The warhead was manufactured in three versions from 1966: WE177A was a boosted-fission device with a variable yield of between 0.5 and 10 kilotons intended to replace "Red Beard," whilst WE177B and WE177C were thermonuclear fusion devices with yields of 450 and 200 kilotons respectively. A total of 319 examples were constructed: 107 of the WE177A variant, 53 of the WE177B and 159 of the WE177C; all had been withdrawn by 1998.

As well as evolving into WE177, RE179 was also developed into the 200-kiloton ET317 warhead, a hybrid fission-fusion-fission version of the US W59 warhead, designed and manufactured by the Atomic Weapons Establishment (AWE) in collaboration with the Americans. This was used to equip British "Polaris" missiles, with subsequent improvements to the warhead made under the code name "Chevaline." When "Trident 2" entered service, ET317 was replaced by a British-produced warhead based on the American W76 with a selective yield of 0.3, 5–10 or 100 kilotons (see Table 3, page 48).

## Abandoned projects

Many British development projects were abandoned before entering production. For example, "Blue Slug," a ship-to-ship guided weapon, was discontinued in 1956, as was "Green Cheese," an air-to-surface anti-ship missile. "Blue Peacock," also known as "Brown Bunny," "Blue Bunny" and "Big Bertha," was a 10-kiloton atomic landmine, but was cancelled in 1957, as was the "Violet Mist" landmine. "Blue Rosette," a free-fall bomb for the Avro 730 bomber, was also discarded in 1957. "Pixie," a lightweight 1-kiloton plutonium device that used cobalt metal pellets as a diagnostic tool for measuring yield, was tested in 1957, but was subsequently abandoned as being too expensive. "Indigo Hammer," a 6-kiloton plutonium implosion device intended for the "Bloodhound" air-defense missile, was axed in 1958. The requirement for a nuclear warhead for "Sea Slug," a naval surface-to-air guided weapon, was cancelled in 1962. And finally, "Yellow Anvil" was a proposed 1-kiloton nuclear artillery shell, scrapped in 1958.

Cancelled British missile projects of the period included "Blue Streak," a medium-range ballistic missile and satellite launch vehicle, which was cancelled in 1960 before reaching production,

**BELOW** "Blue Peacock" was a British atomic landmine with a yield of 10 kilotons, designed to be detonated remotely. Also known as "Brown Bunny," "Blue Bunny" and "Big Bertha," it was cancelled in 1957 without going into production.

*(Warehouse Collection)*

and "Blue Water," a battlefield, or tactical, nuclear weapon of the late 1950s designed to be used against ground troops. "Blue Water" was intended to replace the American "Corporal" system, but was abandoned in 1962.

## Anglo-US development

In 1958, a new US Atomic Energy Act overturned the McMahon Act of 1946 which had outlawed US co-operation on nuclear research with other nations. The new act was proposed by Lewis Strauss, Chairman of the Atomic Energy Commission, and included a clause that allowed the president to share information and research on nuclear weapons and fissile material with allies that were making a "substantial and material contribution to national defense and security" – one such nation was Britain.

Collaboration between the two nations, under a scheme designated Project E, provided Britain with a large number of nuclear weapons, including Mk 5, 7, 28, 43 and 57 free-fall bombs, missiles, naval depth charges, and 8-inch and 155 mm nuclear artillery rounds. The hardware, which started to become available from October 1958, remained under the guardianship of the USA but would have been released for use by British forces had the need arisen, and some US weapons remained available to British forces until the end of the Cold War. As regards delivery vehicles, the lack of success of the "Blue Steel" and "Blue Streak" missiles led to the decision that Britain would adopt the US "Skybolt" missile as a mount for the AWE-designed ET317 warheads. When "Skybolt" was cancelled in 1962, a deal was thrashed out that allowed Britain to deploy American "Polaris," and then "Trident" missiles, albeit with British warheads.

Initially, the missiles were carried in four *Resolution*-class nuclear submarines, each

**RIGHT** During a visit aboard the USS *Observation Island*, US President John F. Kennedy (center) witnessed a demonstration of the firing of a "Polaris A2" ballistic missile from the submarine USS *Andrew Jackson* off the coast of Florida. *(JFK Library)*

**RIGHT** Following the withdrawal of Britain's "Red Snow" warhead, and the cancellation of the US "Skybolt" project, Britain adopted the "Polaris" missile, using a hybrid fission-fusion-fission version of the W59 1-megaton thermonuclear warhead, designated ET317. Initially, the missiles were carried in four *Resolution*-class submarines, each vessel having 16 missiles. *(Warehouse Collection)*

vessel having 16 missiles, armed with a British-built hybrid fission-fusion-fission version of the W59 1-megaton thermonuclear warhead, designated ET317. Each missile could deliver three thermonuclear warheads to a single target. In 1994, the *Resolution*-class submarines were replaced by the new *Vanguard* class, and, at the same time, "Polaris" missiles were superseded by "Trident." Since 1998, "Trident" has been the only operational nuclear weapons system in British service, with warheads, similar to the American W76, constructed by AWE at Aldermaston.

Political debate continues regarding the possible replacement of "Trident."

**LEFT** In 1994, "Polaris" was replaced in British service by the American "Trident," with a British-built warhead similar to the W76. "Trident" was also designed to be launched from a submarine, in this case the USS *Henry M. Jackson*. *(Bob Duff; US Department of Defense)*

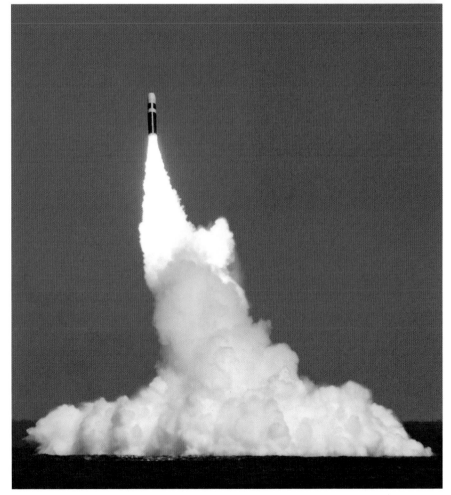

**LEFT** The *Vanguard*-class submarines from which "Trident" is launched are scheduled for replacement before 2030. *(Lockheed Martin)*

LEFT Aerial view of the massive Pantex site located north-east of Amarillo, Texas. The 16,000-acre (6,500-hectare) Pantex plant is the only nuclear weapons assembly and disassembly facility in the USA, currently employing around 3,600 people. *(US Department of Defense)*

CENTER The last example of the 9-megaton Mk 53 (later B53) bomb photographed at Pantex, prior to dismantling. The Mk 53 went into production in 1962 with a total of 340 constructed; it was withdrawn in 1997, and the last one was disassembled on October 25, 2011. *(US National Nuclear Security Administration)*

# Nuclear weapons manufacture

The first American nuclear weapons were produced at the Los Alamos National Laboratory in a modest production facility code-named "Site S"; further production facilities were established at two sites in California, the Naval Ordnance Test Station at China Lake and the Salt Wells Pilot Plant. When production started in earnest, components for "Fat Man" Mk 3 were produced at the Iowa Army Ordnance Plant, at Rock Island Arsenal, and at Salt Wells, the latter site having been the subject of huge expenditure and expansion. The Salt Wells plant closed in 1954, but the National Laboratory at Los Alamos remains active in research and development, along with other organizations. The production of plutonium-239 and uranium-235 currently takes place at the Y-12 National Security Complex in Tennessee, as well as in Ohio and Washington. Tritium, which is essential to the manufacture

LEFT Based at Aldermaston, Berkshire, the AWE has been home to Britain's atomic weapons program since 1950. AWE is responsible for maintaining the warheads for "Trident," designing new atomic weapons, and dismantling and decommissioning redundant warheads. *(Historic England)*

of boosted-fission weapons, was processed at the Savannah River Site, near Aiken, South Carolina, but the production facility was closed down in 1988; the material is still stored on site.

The only current manufacturer of nuclear weapons in the USA is Pantex, based north-east of Amarillo, Texas. Established in 1942 as the last of 14 ordnance plants in Texas, Pantex produced nearly 4 million conventional bombs and artillery shells during the Second World War and was closed the day after the war ended. In 1951, the government acquired the land and production facilities and the plant was reopened as a major nuclear weapons complex. Over the following years, as other similar facilities across the USA closed, Pantex became the primary US location for the assembly, disassembly, retro-fit and modification of nuclear weapons. Describing itself as "the provider of the nuclear deterrent

to the Department of Defense," the plant is currently managed and operated for the US Department of Energy by Consolidated Nuclear Security and Sandia National Laboratories.

Britain's independent nuclear deterrent is produced at what was initially described as the AWRE, located close to the town of Aldermaston, Berkshire. Aspects of the work are also carried out at the Royal Ordnance Factories (ROFs) at Burghfield and Cardiff.

Established on April 1, 1950, at a former RAF base, control of AWRE was passed from the MoS to the newly created UKAEA in 1954. Production activities were transferred to British Nuclear Fuels Limited (BNFL) in 1971, and, in 1987, the activities of ROF Burghfield and ROF Cardiff were combined with AWRE to form the AWE, with the two satellite locations renamed AWE Burghfield and AWE Cardiff. From 1993 to 1999, AWE was operated by Hunting-BRAE,

**ABOVE** Aerial view of the 750-acre (303-hectare) AWE site at Aldermaston; AWE has a second site at nearby Burghfield where warheads are maintained and disassembled. A total of 4,500 staff are employed across the two sites. *(Ivaneol)*

a consortium of Hunting Engineering, Brown and Root, and AEA Technology. The Cardiff site was closed in 1997, and Hunting-BRAE lost the contract to manage the plants in 1999, with control passing to AWE Management Limited, a consortium consisting of BNFL, Lockheed Martin and Serco. A new subsidiary, known as AWE plc, assumed responsibility for the operation of all AWE sites on April 1, 2000, and AWE Aldermaston is currently organized into separate departments for weapons development, warhead physics, warhead design and materials.

Highly enriched weapons-grade uranium was produced at a gaseous diffusion plant at a former ROF at Capenhurst, near Risley, Cheshire. The plant started operation in February 1952, and was producing 275 pounds (125 kg) of highly enriched uranium a year by 1957. Military production ended in 1961 and the plant started producing uranium for use in nuclear power stations.

Weapons-grade plutonium-239 comes from Sellafield in Cumbria, a former ROF facility. The site was closed at the end of the Second World War and passed into commercial ownership, but was subsequently reacquired by the MoS for the production of materials for nuclear weapons. Construction of the processing plant began in September 1947, a task involving some 5,000 workers, and the air-cooled graphite Windscale Piles were completed in July 1950. Within two years, plutonium and uranium were being separated from spent fuel for use in the nuclear weapons program, and it has been estimated that Britain has since produced 8,000 pounds (3,600 kg) of weapons-grade plutonium, with about 850 pounds (385 kg) coming from Windscale. The Piles were shut down following a fire in October 1957 which destroyed the core and released radioactive material into the atmosphere. In 1954, control of the Sellafield site passed to UKAEA, with parts of the operation coming under BNFL in 1971.

# Nuclear stockpiles

Although the majority of the warheads manufactured during the early years of the Cold War were quickly made obsolete by advances in weapons technology, it has been reported that something like 125,000 nuclear warheads have been manufactured since 1945, most of them by either the USA or the Soviet Union. Although neither side could be absolutely certain of the strength of the other, the advantage of numbers was generally with USA until the early 1970s when the first Strategic Arms Limitation Talks (SALT) began. Thousands of warheads have been decommissioned and subsequently destroyed, although it is worth noting that these treaties are concerned only with strategic weapons and not the lower-yield

## TABLE 4 ESTIMATED NUCLEAR STOCKPILES BY NATION

| Nation | Peak warhead | | Current (2016) warhead stockpile |
|---|---|---|---|
| | Stockpile | Date | |
| Britain | 520* | 1975 | 225 |
| China | 434 | n/a | 250 |
| France | 540 | 1992 | 300 |
| India | 110 | 2014 | 110 |
| Israel** | 80 | n/a | 80 |
| North Korea | 20 | 2015 | 20 max*** |
| Pakistan | 120 | 2013 | 120 |
| Soviet Union | approx. 45,000 | 1988 | 7,500**** |
| USA | 31,255 | 1967 | 7,100**** |
| **Total number of nuclear warheads worldwide, 15,705** | | | |

* The British nuclear stockpile peaked at 520 weapons in 1975, but the peak yield occurred in 1967 at 150 megatons.
** Israel has never admitted to having nuclear weapons.
*** Earlier estimates put North Korea's stockpile at ten, but a recent survey by Chinese experts suggests that the figure may be as high as 20.
**** Recent estimates (April 2015) from the Federation of American Scientists, Arms Control Association put these figures at 4,300 and 4,764, respectively.

tactical devices. Whilst it is impossible to pin down the exact number of nuclear weapons that are stockpiled around the world, even today it would appear that there are almost 16,000 viable warheads held by nine countries (see Table 4, page 54).

Weapons stockpiles are generally categorized as either being "active," which means that they are ready for immediate deployment, or "inactive," meaning they are held in some sort of secure storage facility and would require recommissioning before being ready for use. A recent report in the *Daily Telegraph* suggested that both the USA and Russia have something like 2,000 missiles in the "active" category, ready for launch within a maximum of 15 minutes from the order being given.

# Biological and chemical weapons

As though the prospect of all-out nuclear conflict were not bad enough, other "doomsday" devices developed during the Cold War period included chemical and biological weapons designed for mass destruction. Despite the difficulties of manufacture, delivery and storage, such weapons have long been considered useful against civilians and can also be used for what is described as "area denial." Their effects can generally be overcome by the use of proper protective equipment and decontamination measures.

Chemical weapons include: nerve agents such as sarin, cyclosarin and VX; chemicals which have a direct effect on the pulmonary system such as phosgene; skin-blistering agents; blood agents, such as cyanogen chloride; and defoliants. Biological warfare agents – also sometimes described as germ warfare – include bacteria, various toxins, viruses and fungi. Viral herbicides can also be used to destroy an enemy's agriculture. Anthrax is often quoted as meeting the criteria for an effective biological warfare agent and it is certainly extremely toxic; however, as with almost all similar agents, the development of a suitable delivery system remains a problem, as does the difficulty of predicting exactly how long the agent might remain active. When Britain experimentally released anthrax spores on Gruinard Island, off the coast of Scotland during the Second World War, the island was made uninhabitable for decades, with the clean-up process taking eight years.

Since 1993, there has been an international ban on producing and stockpiling chemical weapons under the auspices of the Chemical Weapons Convention, but large stockpiles are known to still exist in several countries including the USA and the former Soviet Union. Similarly, biological warfare, including the production and stockpiling of biological weapons, was outlawed by the 1972 Biological Weapons Convention.

**LEFT** Although the manufacture and stockpiling of chemical and biological weapons are prohibited by international treaties, stocks are known to remain in various countries. This photograph, from 1960, shows a cutaway "Honest John" M190 warhead containing around 350 M134 sarin nerve-agent bomblets. *(US Department of Defense)*

## Chapter Three

# Early warning systems

Throughout the Cold War, NATO and the Warsaw Pact faced each other across the Iron Curtain, each side presuming that the other was only deterred from launching a pre-emptive strike by the prospect of an instant, and deadly, "second-strike" retaliation. However, in order to be in a position to launch a "second strike," it is necessary to know exactly, and in real time, what your enemy is up to.

**OPPOSITE** Work on what was eventually 1,563 ROC underground monitoring posts began in May 1956. The photograph shows the ventilation shafts and equipment post for a typical monitoring post at Lutterworth. *(Nick Catford)*

From 1946 to the mid-1950s, NATO commanders believed that the most likely Cold War scenario involved Soviet bomber aircraft making pre-emptive strikes against cities or manufacturing centers, almost certainly in Europe. Any such strikes would, necessarily, be cataclysmic, and it was essential to maintain vigilance over the actions of the other side by whatever means were available, thus allowing a retaliatory strike to be launched whilst the enemy's missiles were still in the air. An essential component of this vigilance was the electronic early warning system – a chain of passive defense measures, together with the command and control centers that interpreted data received and made decisions regarding retaliation.

Most early warning systems use ground-based radar, but, ultimately, the equipment is also carried in airborne warning and control system (AWACS) aircraft; satellites are also used, in conjunction with infrared detection.

## US early warning systems

**D**uring the Second World War, the USA established a series of perimeter radar installations along the Atlantic and Pacific coasts of Canada and Alaska to provide early warning of any Japanese air attack. Most were abandoned at the end of the war, but, in response to increasing East–West tension, five stations were refurbished to detect Soviet aircraft entering US airspace under what was described as the "radar fence." Further stations

were upgraded as part of a program that was eventually designated Operation Lashup.

A total of 43 stations went into operation in 1950 under the control of Air Defense Command (ADCOM), and, ultimately, 129 radar stations provided coverage across the continental USA. These were supplemented by four concentric arcs of early warning stations described as: the Alaska Radars; the Pinetree Line, the second phase of which was constructed and financed by the Canadian government; the Mid-Canada Line; and the Distant Early Warning Line (DEW), constructed along the edge of Canada's polar ice cap. Although the threat of attack from aircraft had diminished considerably by the end of the 1960s, the DEW was modernized during the 1980s, with a further 15 long-range radar facilities at existing stations. Redesignated the North Warning System, it became operational in 1994, two or three years after the end of the Cold War.

ADCOM became Aerospace Defense Command in 1968 and was broken up in 1979. The atmospheric defense resources, including interceptors, warning radars, and associated bases and personnel, were transferred to Air Defense, Tactical Air Command (ADTAC), while the missile warning and space surveillance assets were transferred to Strategic Air Command, along with control of the USA's land-based bomber aircraft and land-based ballistic missile strategic nuclear arsenal, an arrangement that ended in 1992. ADTAC was

ABOVE DEW Line station at Point Lay, Alaska. *(US Department of Defense)*

RIGHT In 1958, the USA started construction of the advanced BMEWS, which extended as far as Alaska and Greenland. The photograph shows Clear Air Force Station, Alaska. *(US Army Corps of Engineers)*

dismantled in December 1985 and the assets passed to the Air National Guard.

As the threat of aircraft attack became less likely, the possibility of missile attack grew, and, in 1958, RCA (Radio Corporation of America) was contracted to construct an advanced ballistic missile early warning system (BMEWS) extending as far as Alaska and Greenland. Designated 474L – sometimes known as "Big L" – BMEWS comprised a network of 12 stations with radar, computer and communications equipment designed to detect a mass ballistic missile attack directed at the northern approaches of the USA. Construction was completed in 1961, and the system went live during 1962/63, providing a 15- to 25-minute warning for the US military. The scanners were said to have a range of 5,000 miles (8,000 km), and the BMEWS included the iconic domes at the radar station at RAF Fylingdales in North Yorkshire. It was claimed in 1960 that these domes would give the USA an extra 15 minutes' warning – something that was unlikely to benefit Britain!

LEFT Tracker buildings and the distinctive radomes at RAF Fylingdales, North Yorkshire. Constructed in 1962, Fylingdales formed a vital part of the BMEWS. *(Historic England)*

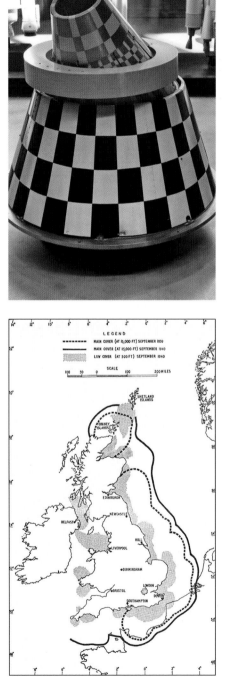

**RIGHT** Dating from 1960, the "Midas" missile defense alarm system employed a series of nine satellites equipped with infrared sensors to provide early warning of the launch of Soviet ICBMs. *(US Department of Defense)*

By 1960, the USA had also established "Midas," a missile defense alarm system relying on a series of satellites that used infrared detection to provide early warning of the launch of Soviet ICBMs; 12 satellites were planned, but, in the end, just 9 were deployed. "Midas" was intended to work in conjunction with the ground-based BMEWS, and, although not generally considered to be a success, the "Midas" program pioneered the technology that led to the development of the Defense Support Program (DSP) from 1970, and the space-based infrared system (SBIRS), the latter including a NATO communications site at RAF Menwith Hill in Yorkshire.

## British early warning systems

**D**uring the first decade of the Cold War, Britain's early warning system consisted of 36 radar stations situated down the eastern and southern edge of the country. Originally part of the "Chain Home" system, the equipment had been installed from about 1936 to detect incoming aircraft, and elements of "Chain Home" continued in use until the mid-1950s. By 1948, the radar stations had been supplemented by 1,420 observation and monitoring posts from which men of the Royal Observer Corps (ROC), under control of RAF Fighter Command, maintained a vigil on the skies across Britain and Northern Ireland. Each ROC post housed three personnel, many of them civil defense volunteers, equipped

**RIGHT** Map showing the coverage of the "Chain Home" system around the British coast in 1939/40. "Chain Home" continued in use until the mid-1950s. *(Warehouse Collection)*

**FAR RIGHT** Surface features of the ROC monitoring post at Soham, Cambridgeshire. *(Historic England)*

| | | |
|---|---|---|
| 1 Ground zero indicator | 4 Air inlet | 10 Loudspeaker telephone |
| 2 Cover for survey meter probe | 5 Telescopic radio aerial | 11 Carrier receiver |
| 3 Baffle plates to bomb-power indicator (BPI) | 6 Radio set | 12 Pneumatic pump for telescopic aerial |
| | 7 BPI | 13 Battery |
| | 8 Fixed survey meter | 14 WC |
| | 9 Radio headset | |

**ABOVE** Cutaway view of a typical ROC monitoring post. *(Warehouse Collection)*

| | |
|---|---|
| 1 blast-proof steel cover | 14 sump access cover |
| 2 drainage pump | 15 WC |
| 3 sump | 16 accumulator cells |
| 4 access ladder | 17 work surface |
| 5 probe for radiation monitor | 18 shelf |
| 6 minimum 3-feet earth cover | 19 probe for radiation monitor |
| 7 pressure gauge | 20 access ladder |
| 8 air-inlet shaft | 21 lighting switch |
| 9 bulletin board | 22 air-inlet shaft |
| 10 work surface | 23 bunk beds |
| 11 communications equipment | 24 storage |
| 12 bunk beds | |
| 13 storage | |

0 1 2 3 4 5 6 feet

**LEFT** Plan and sectional views of a typical ROC monitoring post. *(Bill Padden)*

with simple instruments that could gauge the location and power of a nuclear blast. Incredibly, although many of the posts have now been demolished, elements of the system remained in use until 1991/92.

With the first Soviet test of a nuclear weapon, combined with the increasing speed of enemy bombers, it was clear these somewhat makeshift arrangements could not continue. In the late 1940s, the government began a modernization program for Britain's early warning radar system called "Rotor." In 1949, the Cherry Report proposed that the number of "Chain Home" stations be reduced to 66 and the electronics be upgraded and protected against enemy attack. RAF Fighter Command was rearranged into six operational sectors, and the system was integrated with the Army's anti-aircraft defenses. In August 1952, the Rotor program was assigned "super priority" status, putting it on a par with the development of the nuclear weapons themselves.

The program was carried out in three phases – Rotor 1, Rotor 2 and Rotor 3 – with the majority of the work executed by the Marconi Wireless and Telegraph Company. Rotor 1 consisted of 34 "Chain Home" stations, 8 early warning stations, 11 underground control interception stations and 14 semi-submerged above-ground interception stations. From 1954,

OPPOSITE TOP Typical "Rotor" guardhouse. Some 350,000 tons of concrete, 20,000 tons of steel and thousands of miles of cabling for the telephone and telex connections were used to construct the network of "Rotor" bunkers, radar installations, and command and control centers. *(Bill Padden)*

OPPOSITE BOTTOM Typical "Rotor 3" operations room. Designed to detect aircraft as small as a jet fighter at a range of 200 miles (320 km) and an altitude of 50,000 feet (15,240 km), "Rotor 3" would have extended coverage across Northern Ireland, and the north and north-west of Scotland, but was never completed. *(Bill Padden)*

ABOVE Headquarters building for ROC number 15 group at Fiskerton, Lincolnshire. The building was commissioned in 1960 and closed in 1992. *(Nick Catford)*

RIGHT Headquarters building for ROC number 7 group at Bedford. Note the near identical construction to the Fiskerton building: both feature a semi-underground design. *(Historic England)*

Rotor 2 saw the new "Green Garlic" Type 80 radar system installed on 29 existing sites. It was never fully completed, but Rotor 3 would have extended coverage across Northern Ireland and the north and north-west of Scotland, allowing even fighter aircraft to be detected at a range of 200 miles (320 km) and an altitude of 50,000 feet (15,240 km). Rotor 4 consisted of sector operational command (SOC) sites at Barnton Quarry, Bawburgh, Kelvedon Hatch and Shipton. Work on Rotor ended in 1956.

Advances in jamming techniques, and the emergence of other electronic countermeasures (ECM), suggested that new radar equipment would be necessary to continue to provide adequate early warning of attack. In February 1961, what had originally been described as "Plan Ahead" was approved for deployment under the name "Linesman." The new system was to be integrated with civil air-traffic control, with elements of the latter designated "Mediator." The new, more-powerful Marconi Type 84 radar equipment was installed at three

LEFT Guardhouse and entrance to the bunker at Kelvedon Hatch, Essex. Decommissioned in 1992, the bunker served initially as an air-defense station before being converted to a "Rotor 4" site in 1953, and subsequently served as a Regional Seat of Government (RSG). The standard design of the guardhouse can also be seen at other, similar, sites. *(Nick Catford)*

1 covered veranda
2 guard room
3 armory
4 storage area
5 rest room
6 WC
7 WC
8 blast-proof doors

9 reinforced roof slab
10 water tank
11 guard room
12 steel-shuttered windows
13 covered veranda
14 corridor to lower levels

section at A-A

1 equipment well
2 storage area
3 equipment well
4 access
5 transformer chamber
6 cable duct
7 radar room
8 radar room
9 workshop
10 control room
11 office
12 WC
13 WC
14 telecommunications equipment
15 ventilation equipment
16 rest room
17 rest room
18 switchgear
19 frequency converters
20 sump and drainage pump
21 chillers
22 filtration equipment
23 emergency exit

section at A-A

section at B-B

**ABOVE** "Rotor 1" consisted of 34 "Chain Home" stations, 8 early warning stations, 11 underground control interception stations and 14 semi-submerged above-ground interception stations. The drawing shows a typical "Rotor 1" operations room. *(Bill Padden)*

**BELOW** "Rotor 4" sector operational command (SOC) installation. "Rotor 4" sites were at Barnton Quarry, Bawburgh, Kelvedon Hatch and Shipton. *(Bill Padden)*

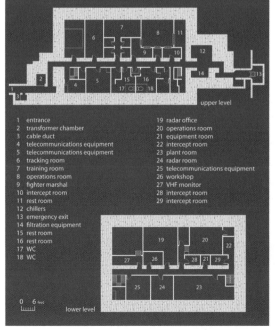

upper level

1 entrance
2 transformer chamber
3 cable duct
4 telecommunications equipment
5 telecommunications equipment
6 tracking room
7 training room
8 operations room
9 fighter marshal
10 intercept room
11 rest room
12 chillers
13 emergency exit
14 filtration equipment
15 rest room
16 rest room
17 WC
18 WC
19 radar office
20 operations room
21 equipment room
22 intercept room
23 plant room
24 radar room
25 telecommunications equipment
26 workshop
27 VHF monitor
28 intercept room
29 intercept room

lower level

1 blast-proof doors
2 entrance corridor
3 transformer chamber
4 operations room
5 chillers
6 blast-proof doors
7 filtration equipment
8 emergency exit
9 plant room
10 air outlet duct

ABOVE Marconi Linesman Type 84 radar array at RAF Neatishead, Norfolk. Replacing the earlier Rotor system, Linesman operated on a wavelength of 230 mm using a 60-foot- (18.3-m-) wide antenna reflector. The transmitting equipment was contained in the building on which the aerial was mounted.
*(Warehouse Collection)*

sites, in Norfolk, Northumberland and North Yorkshire. Unlike the earlier Rotor system, Linesman incorporated central control using a mainframe computer operating across a local area network.

By 1968, the further-improved AEI "Blue Yeoman" Type 85 radar, designed to deter hostile jamming by rapidly changing

frequencies, was installed at all three stations, complete with heavy-duty cooling equipment. Linesman was finally declared fully operational in 1974, by which time it was considered to be vulnerable to Soviet stand-off missiles. By this time, NATO had moved away from the so-called "tripwire" response, typified by Rotor and Linesman, and was investigating a more flexible warning system incorporating both deterrent and defense components.

In 1971, a NATO report entitled "A Revised Plan for the UKADGE," proposed centralizing command at West Drayton and High Wycombe, with control and reporting centers at RAF Buchan (Scotland), Neatishead (Norfolk), Bishops Court (Northern Ireland) and Boulmer (Northumberland). At the same time, early warning radar and control systems were deployed in Shackleton aircraft based at Kinloss and Lossiemouth in Scotland to provide "over-the-horizon" coverage. The ground sites were linked by a narrow-band digital ring main that allowed one station to provide backup should others suffer technical problems or be damaged by enemy action, while the UK Air Defence Ground Environment (UKADGE) system was fully integrated with the wider NATO Air Defence Ground Environment (NADGE) system.

By 1972, the NADGE system had evolved into the NATO Integrated Air Defense System

RIGHT Element of the war telephone system at RAF Neatishead; this is the equipment that would have been used to issue the "four-minute warning."
*(Warehouse Collection)*

**ABOVE** Standard local early warning and control (SLEWC) consoles and tote board at RAF Neatishead. *(Nick Catford)*

**RIGHT** The Marconi S600 transportable long-range radar system was designed for early warning and surveillance, control of surface-to-air missiles, coast watching and military air-traffic control. The equipment could be air-lifted by helicopter, loaded into transport aircraft such as the C130 or towed by a Land Rover. *(Warehouse Collection)*

(NATINADS), consisting of 84 radar sites and associated control centers across Europe, including sites in Britain. This, in turn, became the airborne early warning/ground environment integration segment (AEGIS) in the early 1980s, assembling and interpreting data derived from both AWACS and NATINADS into visual displays.

**RIGHT** Staxton Wold was first used as a radar station in 1937, as part of the "Chain Home" system, and is the oldest continuously serving radar station in the world. The station was one of those equipped with Type 84 radar, but, by 1996, this had been removed and replaced with Plessey Type 93 equipment removed from RAF Hopton. *(Nick Catford)*

# "Pressing the nuclear button"

**W**hile it is one thing developing an effective early warning system, it is quite another to react to the data received and to actually "press the nuclear button."

In the USA, the President has the final say over the deployment of nuclear weapons, with the launch codes of what is described as the Single Integrated Operational Plan on hand at all times. The President is always accompanied by a military aide who carries the so-called "nuclear football," a name dating back to Eisenhower's time, and an attack plan code-named Operation Dropkick. The "football" is actually a small leather briefcase containing a book listing classified site locations, a description of procedures for the Emergency Alert System that allows the President to address the nation and a small plastic card on which are printed the authentication codes – described as the "Gold Codes" – required to launch a strike. The launch codes, and the equipment used for decrypting them, are generated daily by the National Security Agency.

The orders to retaliate against any perceived Soviet threat would be issued through one of the USA's underground command, control and communications centers. Six of these facilities were constructed during the 1950s as part of a program that also included a network of nuclear-bomb-proof bunkers to protect the major figures in the administration. The largest of these was the NORAD headquarters buried deep in the Cheyenne Mountain complex at Colorado Springs. From 1974, there was also an airborne command center, designated "Looking Glass," operating from a fleet of four modified Boeing 747 "Night Watch" airliners. A similar ground-based system is located at the National Airborne Operations Center at Offutt Air Force Base, Omaha, and there was an underground complex at Raven Rock Mountain in Pennsylvania, often described as the "underground Pentagon."

Unless coordination with the US Strategic Air Command is required, Britain's deterrent is under the control of the Prime Minister, through the Chief of the Defence Staff. By 1957, Britain had identified a list of 131 Soviet cities with a population exceeding 100,000, of which 98 had been selected as legitimate targets. Should the moment have arrived, the Prime Minister, or his designated survivor, would have issued the order, known as the "letter of last resort," which, for much of the Cold War period, would have come from the underground bunker complex at Corsham, Wiltshire, known as "Burlington." Should an attack have been deemed likely, a defined protocol allowed a civil servant to speak to the Prime Minister, whose responses would have been either: to retaliate, to not retaliate, for the commander to use his own judgement or to place himself under US or Australian command if possible.

By the end of the Cold War era, Britain had two control and reporting centers, one at Buchan, the other at Neatishead. These centers reported to the UK Combined Air Operations Centre at RAF High Wycombe where Strike Command headquarters was located until 2007. However, any orders to launch a "Trident" strike from the British *Vanguard* submarine fleet would have been relayed to the operations room at the British military headquarters at Northwood, Hertfordshire, where the Chief of the Defence Staff would have "pressed the button."

Exactly how the Soviet Union might have issued any orders to launch nuclear weapons remains unclear, but, since 1967, the Soviets are said to have developed an automatic "trigger system" – often described as a "Doomsday machine" – that would launch ballistic missiles if a nuclear strike were to be detected by seismic, light, radioactivity and overpressure sensors. Code-named "Dead

**ABOVE** The bunker in which the NORAD headquarters is located is designed to withstand a 30-megaton nuclear blast within 1.2 miles (2 km). Sets of 25-ton blast-resistant doors are used to protect the access tunnels. *(USAF)*

Hand," or "Perimeter," this would allow the Soviets to maintain a retaliatory second-strike capability even if all of the High Command, and the Soviet underground command and control network deep under Moscow, had been incapacitated. Some small comfort can perhaps be gained from the fact that the system was only to have been made active during periods of heightened tension.

**BELOW** Photographed in May 1999, these are the vandalized remains of the guardhouse to the "Rotor 1" station at Bempton, Yorkshire, which was commissioned in 1956. *(Nick Catford)*

## Chapter Four

# Air-launched nuclear weapons

Hiroshima and Nagasaki were attacked from the air using free-fall bombs, and for the next decade aircraft provided the only feasible means of delivery for strategic nuclear weapons. Both sides constructed long-range heavy bombers capable of delivering a nuclear payload across a distance, and maintained a fleet of such aircraft ready to fly at short notice.

*"Someday, not too distant, there can come streaking out of somewhere – we won't be able to hear it, it will come so fast – some kind of gadget with an explosive so powerful that one projectile will be able to wipe out completely this city of Washington."*

**General Hap Arnold, US Army, 1943**

**OPPOSITE** Making its maiden flight in August 1952, the iconic Vulcan bomber provided the means of delivering Britain's nuclear deterrent from July 1956 to June 1969, when the role passed to the "Polaris"-equipped submarines of the Royal Navy. *(Sergeant David S. Nolan; USAF)*

the long-range bomber, and, although the USA, Russia and China all continue to maintain a fleet of strategic bombers, the British V-Bombers had all been withdrawn from service by the mid-1980s, with the last remaining examples converted to air-to-air refuelling tankers.

# The British V-Bombers

D evelopment of Britain's V-Bomber fleet – the Vulcan, Valiant and Victor – started in January 1947, when the Air Ministry issued a specification for an advanced jet-powered, medium-range bomber that could carry one 10,000-pound (4,535 kg) bomb to a target 1,720 miles (2,775 km) away. The specification stated the aircraft must have a cruising speed of 575 mph (925 km/h), and be capable of flying at a ceiling of 50,000 feet (15,200 m).

**ABOVE Entering service with USAF Strategic Air Command in 1955, the Boeing B-52 Stratofortress is a long-range, subsonic, jet-powered strategic bomber constructed to carry nuclear weapons, and designed to provide a first strike or retaliation capability.** *(US Department of Defense)*

All of Britain's independent nuclear weapons, including "Blue Danube," "Red Beard," "Yellow Sun" and WE177, were free-fall bombs, designed to be dropped from the V-Bomber fleet. During periods of heightened tension, the USA kept squadrons of B-52 Stratofortress aircraft airborne around the clock, flying across the Atlantic to the coast of Europe and back, ready to retaliate against the Soviet Union.

Soviet bombers, including the Tupolev Tu-4 and the later Tu-16, described by NATO as "Bull" and "Badger," respectively, maintained the ability to strike against distant targets in Europe and the USA. The Chinese produced a licensed version of the Tu-16, known as the Xian H-6, equally capable of delivering nuclear weapons across thousands of miles. But, by the end of the 1950s, the development of more capable ICBMs had started to usurp the role of

Handley Page and Avro both responded with innovative designs. The Handley Page Victor featured crescent wings, while the Avro Vulcan used an even more advanced, visually striking, delta-wing arrangement with no tail-plane. Both companies received development contracts, the thinking being that if one of these advanced designs failed, the other would serve as useful insurance, and work on the two aircraft began at the end of 1947. A third, more conventional aircraft, the Vickers Valiant, was also commissioned in April 1948, following a less-demanding specification. Production of the three aircraft – collectively described as the V-Bomber force – started in the 1950s, with the intention of producing a fleet of 144 aircraft that could "strike a worthwhile blow against our enemies," or, as the 1954 "Statement on Defence" put it, would be "capable of using the atomic weapons to the fullest effect."

By the middle of the next decade, Bomber Command had V-Bomber bases across the country, with the aircraft able to reach targets in the east of the Soviet Union, and in Warsaw Pact countries, in the shortest possible time. Valiants were stationed at RAF Marham, although they were soon withdrawn due to technical problems; there were nine Vulcan squadrons, at Cottesmore, Waddington and Scampton; and four Victor squadrons, at Honington, Wittering and Finningley, the latter a training unit. During the 1970s, there were

**BELOW Serving the Soviet Air Force between 1954 and 1993, the Tupolev Tu-16, code-named "Badger" by NATO, was a twin-engined long-range strategic bomber designed to carry either free-fall bombs or air-launched nuclear or conventional cruise missiles.** *(US Department of Defense)*

also Vulcan nuclear squadrons at RAF Akrotiri in Cyprus, although by this time responsibility for Britain's nuclear deterrent had theoretically passed to the Royal Navy.

For two decades, the RAF took its role as the defender of Britain extremely seriously, maintaining aircraft at a high state of readiness.

## Vickers Valiant

Despite the fact that work on the Vickers Valiant B1 had started last, it was the first of the new strategic jet-powered bombers to take to the air, making its maiden flight on May 18, 1951. Designed for a crew of five, consisting of the pilot and co-pilot, air electronics officer (AEO), navigator radar officer and navigator plotter, the Valiant was capable of carrying 21,000 pounds (9,535 kg) of conventional weapons, or a single 10,000-pound (4,535 kg) free-fall nuclear weapon such as "Blue Danube" or "Red Beard," or the American Mks 5, 7, 15, 28 and 43 nuclear bombs. Four Rolls-Royce Avon jet engines were buried in the wing root, and the Valiant was able to deliver its payload across 4,500 miles (7,245 km) – more than enough to get to the heart of the Soviet Union and back from bases in Britain. Maximum speed was 567 mph (913 km/h), and the aircraft had an operating ceiling of 49,000 feet (14,700 m).

The Valiant entered service in 1955, with a total of 100 examples constructed. There were four sub-variants, including photo-reconnaissance aircraft, which entered service in 1955, and in-flight refuelling tankers, the first of these entering service a year later, in

1956; seven Valiants carried ECM equipment. In 1956, during Operation Buffalo, a Valiant dropped the first British nuclear weapon at the Maralinga site that formed part of the Woomera range in Australia. A year later, in 1957, during Operation Grapple, a Valiant tanker was adapted to drop "Short Green Granite," Britain's first thermonuclear (hydrogen) bomb, at Malden Island and Christmas Island in the Central Pacific Ocean.

By 1960, it was not possible for aircraft to fly high enough to avoid interception and the RAF's strategy changed to low-level bombing. The Valiant proved unable to withstand the additional stresses imposed by low-level flying, and was withdrawn in 1965, when fatigue cracks were discovered in the main wing spar.

## Avro Vulcan

Designed by Roy Chadwick and Stuart Davies, the prototype Avro 698, later to become the Vulcan, made its maiden flight on August 30, 1952. The first production example, the Vulcan B1, flew on February 4, 1955, and the type entered service in May 1956.

**ABOVE The Vickers Valiant was the first V-Bomber to enter service with the RAF, but, like the Victor, it was withdrawn prematurely from its intended role when fatigue cracks started to appear in the main wing spar.**
*(Air Team Images)*

**LEFT WZ391 was one of 11 examples of the Valiant photo-reconnaissance aircraft, and served with 543 Squadron at RAF Gaydon. The aircraft was photographed at the Battle of Britain at Home Display at Edinburgh in 1958, two years after delivery.**
*(Air Team Images)*

The unmistakeable delta-wing shape of the Avro Vulcan, in this case a B2 variant, showing the low-level glossy Medium Sea Grey and Dark Green disruptive pattern camouflage that was adopted for the upper surfaces from the mid-1960s. *(Air Team Images)*

**BELOW** Finally retired at the end of the 2015 season, Vulcan XH558 was the last surviving airworthy example of this fine aircraft. It was also the last Vulcan to fly in military service and was one of six Vulcans converted to the aerial refuelling tanker role. *(Air Team Images)*

The prototype was powered by four Bristol Avon jet engines, but once production of the B1 variant started, these were changed to Bristol (later Rolls-Royce) Olympus engines, providing almost double the power. Late production variants had a maximum speed of 644 mph (1,038 km/h), a service ceiling of 55,000 feet (16,775 m) and a range of 2,607 miles (4,171 km). The wing of the prototypes, and of the B1 variant, was a pure delta shape, but when the improved Vulcan B2 appeared in 1960, this had been changed to a compound design, often described as the "kinked wing." Operated by a crew of five, the Vulcan was a very capable aircraft, and it was said to be able to outmaneuver an F-15 fighter in a high-altitude mock dogfight.

Production of the Vulcan continued until 1965, with a total of 136 examples constructed, including two prototypes, and the type formed the backbone of Britain's airborne nuclear deterrent for much of the Cold War, carrying "Blue Danube," "Violet Club" and "Yellow Sun" Mk 1 or Mk 2 free-fall nuclear bombs. The Vulcan was also capable of carrying conventional weapons. There were 45 examples of the B1, 30 of which were subsequently

**LEFT** The Vulcan was capable of carrying "Blue Danube," "Green Grass," Mk 5, "Red Beard," "Violet Club," "Yellow Sun" and WE177 nuclear weapons. The aircraft could also deploy the "Blue Steel" stand-off missile following modifications to the bomb bay. *(US Department of Defense)*

converted to carry ECM equipment; these started to enter service in 1960. The remaining aircraft were of B2 configuration, 24 of which were subsequently converted to carry the "Blue Steel" 1.1-megaton air-launched stand-off missile. The conversion entailed cutting away the bomb-bay doors, as well as various internal modifications, but these aircraft were withdrawn and converted back to B2 configuration in 1970 when the use of "Blue Steel" was discontinued. Four B2 variants were converted for maritime radar reconnaissance in 1973, and, in 1982, six B2s were rebuilt as air-to-air refuelling tankers, with fuel tanks in the bomb bay.

Early production examples were finished in silver, but this was changed to an anti-flash white paint to help reflect the thermal radiation from a nuclear explosion. However, the possible effects of nuclear flash, of both light and heat, on the crew remained a very real issue. In a slightly surreal official film, the crew are shown wearing single eye-patches: if the initial brilliant flash of light produced by the nuclear detonation resulted in blindness of the exposed eye, whether permanent or temporary, the patch could be removed and the pilot could continue to fly the aircraft using the other eye. Anti-flash goggles were subsequently developed to provide better protection.

With the introduction of a low-level attack strategy in the mid-1960s, many aircraft were refinished with a glossy disruptive camouflage pattern on the upper surfaces, consisting of a sea-grey background with dark green stripes. The undersurfaces generally remained white,

although, in 1979, a number of aircraft were painted an all-over camouflage pattern.

The Vulcan was used operationally on just one occasion, during the Falklands War in 1982, and the last examples were withdrawn from service in 1984. One airworthy aircraft has survived – although it ceased flying at the end of 2015 due to the high cost of maintenance.

## Handley Page Victor

Designed by Reginald Stafford, the Handley Page HP80 Victor was the third, and most advanced, of the V-Bombers, readily identified by its crescent wings, thick wing roots and distinctive air intakes. The prototype made its maiden flight on Christmas Eve 1952. The first production example flew on February 1, 1956. The aircraft entered service at the end of 1957, and a total of 84 examples were constructed before the production line was closed down in

**ABOVE** "Blue Steel" air-to-surface nuclear stand-off missile being offloaded from its AEC Mandator transporter vehicle on to a trailer that will allow it to be maneuvered under an aircraft for loading. The missile required up to seven hours of launch preparation, with refuelling alone taking some 30 minutes, and it was said to be highly unreliable.
*(IWM, RAF-T 4863)*

**LEFT** "Blue Steel" missile being readied for loading under a Vulcan bomber; the size of the missile prevented it fitting inside the bomb bay and it was carried under the fuselage. Entering service in 1963, the missile carried a "Red Snow" thermonuclear warhead with a yield of 1.1 megatons, and was finally retired in 1970.
*(IWM, RAF-T 4855)*

**ABOVE** The Handley Page Victor was designed to carry "Blue Danube" and "Yellow Sun" weapons; like the Vulcan, it could also be converted to carry a single underslung "Blue Steel" stand-off missile. *(Air Team Images)*

1963. Like the Vulcan and the Valiant, the Victor was capable of carrying either a conventional payload, in this case in the form of thirty-five 1,000-pound (450 kg) bombs, or a single "Blue Danube." The bomb bay was sufficiently large to be able to carry four of the later "Red Beard," "Yellow Sun" Mk 1 or Mk 2 bombs.

In its early B1 form, the Victor was powered by four Armstrong-Siddeley Sapphire jet engines, but, by the time the improved B2 variant, with its extended wingspan, appeared in 1961, the engines were Rolls-Royce Conway units, with a Blackburn Artouste auxiliary engine in the right-hand wing root. Capable of operating at a ceiling of 56,000 feet (17,080 m), the B1 variant had a maximum speed of 626 mph (300 km/h), and a range of 6,000 miles (9,720 km).

A total of 84 Victors were constructed, 50 of the original B1 configuration, with the remainder being the later B2. Numbers of

**CENTER** Making its first flight in 1952, and entering service in 1958, the Victor was the last of the three V-Bombers. It was withdrawn from the nuclear role in 1968, when fatigue cracks were discovered in the wing structure, exacerbated by use of the aircraft as a low-level bomber. *(Air Team Images)*

**LEFT** A total of 84 Victors were constructed, 50 of which were of the original B1 variant, the remainder being the more powerful B2, which can be recognized by its larger air intakes. *(Air Team Images)*

**ABOVE** Although it was withdrawn from use as a strategic nuclear bomber in 1968, many Victors were converted to the refuelling role, and the type was the last of the V-Bombers to be retired. The final example remained in service until October 15, 1993. *(US Department of Defense)*

aircraft were subsequently converted to the strategic reconnaissance and refuelling tanker roles, with a number of these taking part in both the Falklands Campaign and the first Gulf War; 21 aircraft also had the bomb-bay doors cut away to accommodate a "Blue Steel" air-launched missile.

Although it was withdrawn from the nuclear strike role in 1968 due to the appearance of fatigue cracks, the Victor was the last of the V-Bombers to remain in service, with the final examples withdrawn in 1993. Five remain on display at various air museums although none are flightworthy.

## Other nuclear-capable aircraft

Mention should also be made of the English Electric Canberra, a fast, high-altitude jet-engined bomber powered by Rolls-Royce Avon engines, capable of delivering its payload across a range of 2,000 miles (3,250 km). The Canberra entered service in 1951, with the last example retired in 1972, but it lacked the ability to operate against the Soviet Union from bases in Britain, when it was outside the range of Gee, the navigational radar system. Nevertheless, four squadrons of Canberras based in Germany carried American Mk 7, and later Mk 43, bombs, whilst three squadrons at Akrotiri in Cyprus, and a single squadron in Singapore, were armed with "Red Beard." The size of the Canberra and its bomb bay had precluded the use of early nuclear weapons, but the aircraft

**ABOVE** Loading trials for "Yellow Sun" Mk 2 into a Victor bomber; 1962, Farnborough. *(RAF Museum, Crown Copyright)*

**ABOVE** Prototype for the English Electric Canberra, a fast, high-altitude bomber capable of carrying "Red Beard," Mk 7 and Mk 43 nuclear weapons. *(Ministry of Defence)*

**LEFT** The Canberra entered service in 1951 and was retired in 1972, with nuclear-capable Canberras operated out of RAF Akrotiri and Singapore. *(Warehouse Collection)*

ABOVE **Introduced in 1961, "Red Beard" was a free-fall tritium-boosted fission bomb, with a yield of 15–25 kilotons. The weapon is seen here loaded into the belly of a Blackburn Buccaneer.** (RAF Museum, Crown Copyright)

was also capable of delivering a conventional bomb load of up to 10,000 pounds (4,545 kg).

The Blackburn Buccaneer, which entered service in 1968, was also nuclear capable, carrying the "Red Beard" or WE177A weapons, whilst, towards the end of the Cold War, both the Jaguar GR1 and its replacement, the Tornado GR1, were also considered capable of delivering the WE177C.

# V-Bomber airfields

**B**ritain's expenditure on the V-Bomber fleet was accompanied by a massive investment in airfield infrastructure from the mid- to late 1950s onwards. By the end of

the decade, there were ten "Class 1" main airfields, located in a large semicircle centered on the Wash, each with an allocation of three squadrons of eight V-Bombers. In addition, 36 sites across the country, including five in Scotland and two in Northern Ireland, were identified as "dispersal" bases, designed to allow aircraft to escape the effects of an enemy attack on the main bases. Each dispersal base had an allocation of either two or four aircraft according to the facilities available. By 1962, the number of dispersal sites had been reduced to 32 (see Table 5, page 77).

Nine of the main V-Bomber airfields included storage facilities for up to a dozen nuclear weapons, but, during the 1950s and early '60s, should a crisis have arisen, additional weapons were available from storage sites at RAF Barnham in Suffolk, and at RAF Faldingworth, Lincolnshire.

## Main bases

With the exception of RAF Gaydon in Warwickshire, which had been a temporary airfield constructed in 1942, the main V-Bomber bases were developed from pre-war facilities. The pattern of work required to accommodate the heavy aircraft varied from one site to another, but the most significant change was the provision of a new concrete runway, 200 feet (61 m) in width and 9,000 feet (2,743 m) in length, capable of supporting aircraft up to 89 tons (90,620 kg) in weight. Construction of these new runways often required the realignment of public roads running close to the airfield perimeter. Large hangars were also constructed, together with buildings and earth-protected structures – described as "unit stores" – for storing and assembling nuclear weapons. The sites included avionics facilities, air-traffic control, stores, a briefing block, flight simulator, and crew accommodation and barracks. There was also new provision for the bulk storage of fuel, and the airfields were defended by "Bloodhound" surface-to-air missiles.

Gaydon required considerably more work, including the construction of completely new hangars, and similar buildings were also built at RAF Wittering, near Peterborough.

Quick reaction to any perceived threat was considered to be vital, and, from 1957,

RIGHT **The last line of defense in the protection of the V-Bomber bases was the Bristol "Bloodhound" surface-to-air missile, replacing the earlier "Thunderbird." The "Bloodhound" served from 1958 to 1991.** (Warehouse Collection)

two levels of readiness were defined. At the "strategic" level, three-quarters of the force was made ready for notice of take-off within 24 hours, while the "tactical" level required aircraft at 15-minute readiness for a maximum of seven days, and 40-minute readiness for a month. This was achieved by constructing a large concrete dispersal area, later described as an "operational readiness platform" (ORP), which minimized take-off time by placing up to four aircraft close to the runways. From the beginning of 1962, it was decided to extend the 15-minute readiness across the entire V-Bomber force. Special "quick reaction alert" (QRA) hangars were constructed, with self-contained crew accommodation, further reducing reaction time, and one aircraft from each squadron was held at 15 minutes' readiness, 365 days a year. Once the crew were strapped into their seats it was said the aircraft could be in the air within three to four minutes; it has even been claimed a Vulcan could be airborne in under two minutes.

The need to maintain the V-Bomber QRA capability came to an end in June 1969, when the Royal Navy "Polaris" force became operational, but many of the airfields were upgraded with hardened aircraft shelters (HAS) during the 1980s, providing enhanced protection for both aircraft and personnel.

## Dispersal bases

In times of heightened international tension, the V-Bomber bases would be prime enemy targets: by knocking out airfields, the capacity to strike back is neutralized so, to avoid the risk of aircraft being destroyed on the ground, from 1958 a series of "dispersal airfields" were constructed. These allowed the bombers, already loaded with their nuclear weapons, to be moved to a safe location where they could be kept at a few minutes' readiness. There was a maximum of 36 of these bases at any given time, but not always at the same locations. Each had a runway of a similar length to the main bases, as well as, often rudimentary, crew accommodation. There were no facilities for off-loading or storing nuclear weapons.

The dispersal bases were generally only used during training exercises, which means that the aircraft were loaded with "practice inert" bombs.

**ABOVE** **Gaydon-type prefabricated steel V-Bomber hangar, constructed during August and September 1952 at RAF Wittering as part of the NATO strategic airborne nuclear deterrent. The hangar currently has Grade II listed building status.** *(Historic England)*

**BELOW** **Type D1 earth-mounded building at RAF Finningley where "Blue Danube," "Red Beard" and other bombs were taken for assembly before being moved to the so-called "special weapons" stores.** *(Historic England)*

## TABLE 5 V-BOMBER MAIN AND DISPERSAL AIRFIELDS, FEBRUARY 1962

| Main airfields | RAF Coningsby, Cottesmore, Finningley, Gaydon, Honington, Marham, Scampton, Waddington, Wittering, Wyton |
|---|---|
| Dispersal airfields | RAF Aldergrove, Ballykelly, Bedford, Boscombe Down, Brawdy, Bruntingthorpe, Burtonwood, Carnaby, Coltishall, Cranwell, Elvington, Filton, Kemble, Kinloss, Leconfield, Leeming, Leuchars, Llanbedr, Lossiemouth, Lyneham, Macrihanish, Manston, Middleton St. George, Pershore, Prestwick, Shawbury, St. Mawgan, Stansted, Tarrant Rushton, Valley, Wattisham, Yeovilton |
| Nuclear weapons stores | RAF Barnham, Faldingworth |

## TABLE 6 BRITISH NUCLEAR-STRIKE AIRCRAFT

| Aircraft | Date in service | Types of bomb carried |
|---|---|---|
| Avro Shackleton | 1951 | Mk 34 "Lulu" |
| Avro Vulcan B Mk 1, Mk 1A | 1956 | "Blue Danube"; "Green Grass"; Mk 5*; "Red Beard"; "Violet Club"; "Yellow Sun" Mk 1, Mk 2 |
| B Mk 2, Mk 2A | 1958 | "Blue Steel"; WE1771A; WE177B; "Yellow Sun" Mk 2 |
| Blackburn Buccaneer S1, S2 | 1962 | "Red Beard", WE177A |
| British Aerospace Sea Harrier FRS1 | 1978 | WE177A |
| English Electric Canberra B(I) Mk 8 | 1956 | Mk 5*; Mk 7*; Mk 43* |
| B Mk 15, Mk 16 | 1962 | "Red Beard" |
| Handley Page Victor B Mk 1, Mk 1A | 1957 | "Blue Danube"; "Yellow Sun" Mk 1, Mk 2 |
| B2 | 1962 | "Blue Steel" |
| Hawker Siddeley Nimrod R1 | 1969 | B57* |
| Panavia Tornado GR1 | 1979 | WE177A; WE177C |
| SEPECAT Jaguar GR1 | 1974 | WE177A; WE177C |
| Supermarine Scimitar F1 | 1957 | "Red Beard" |
| Vickers Valiant B Mk 1 | 1955 | B2*; "Blue Danube"; Mk 5*; Mk 7*; Mk 15*; Mk 28*; Mk 43*; "Red Beard" |
| **Helicopters** | | |
| Westland Wessex HAS1 | 1961 | WE177A |
| Wasp HAS1 | 1963 | WE177A |
| Sea King HAR3A | 1969 | WE177A |
| Lynx WG.13 | 1978 | WE177A |

* Indicates weapons of US origin.

However, during the Cuban Missile Crisis of 1962, loaded Vulcan bombers were lined up on the runways with their engines running, ready to take off with just minutes' notice for their targets in the Soviet Union.

## Weapons stores

Purpose-designed maintenance and storage facilities were constructed at RAF Barnham between 1953 and 1959, for the "Blue Danube" weapons. The cobalt and plutonium fissile

**RIGHT** One of 57 "Type A" brick-built hutches at RAF Barnham designed to store the fissile core of the "Blue Danube" weapon. *(Warehouse Collection)*

cores and the casings were stored separately. For the fissile cores, 57 small brick and concrete kiosks were constructed, known as "hutches" or "igloos": 48 "Type A" hutches, each holding a single core, and nine "Type B" hutches, each holding two cores. Combination locks were fitted to the hutches to prevent unauthorized access, and each core was stored in a 2-foot (610 mm) deep, lidded stainless-steel vessel set into a borehole in the solid concrete floor. The maximum storage capacity was 64 cores, although it seems that this was never reached.

The casings, the high-explosive components and other non-nuclear items were kept in three larger brick-built buildings, protected by earth banking. Each was provided with a 10-ton lifting gantry for handling the large and heavy "Blue Danube" bombs – the casing was 24 feet (7.32 m) long and 60 inches (1,524 mm) in diameter, and the complete weapon weighed 10,000 pounds (4,636 kg). The facility also included maintenance areas, a fire station, guardroom and an administration block.

Although Barnham was some way from the V-Bomber airfields, the site supplied assembled weapons to RAF Cottesmore, Gaydon, Honington, Marham, Waddington, Wittering and Wyton. However, within less than a decade it had become obvious that nuclear-weapon storage facilities should be provided at the airfields themselves. The "hutches" at Barnham were decommissioned in 1963, and the property was sold in 1966. Parts have been redeveloped, but some of the original buildings and kiosks remain, and the site has been scheduled as a monument by Historic England.

**ABOVE LEFT** Inside each hutch, the fissile core was stored in a stainless-steel vessel cast into the concrete floor slab. The building was protected by a combination lock, but the heavy counterbalanced lid to the storage vessel had nothing more than a simple cam lock. *(Warehouse Collection)*

**ABOVE** The "Type B" hutches at Barnham, of which there were nine, included provision for storing two fissile cores. *(Warehouse Collection)*

Similar storage and maintenance facilities were also constructed at a former heavy bomber base at RAF Faldingworth, Lincolnshire, in 1957, to supply the northern V-Bomber bases at Coningsby, Finningley and Scampton.

**BELOW** RAF Barnham is now a small industrial estate, but the hutches and many of the other buildings, including the three earth-protected structures where the high-explosive components and other non-nuclear items were stored, still remain. *(Warehouse Collection)*

The site started to be run down from 1968, and was deactivated by 1972; it is currently used as an industrial estate.

By 1964, the standard British nuclear bomb was the WE177. Physically smaller than previous weapons, WE177 was manufactured in three variants, and was stored, assembled and maintained on the V-Bomber bases in earth-covered concrete "special weapons" stores on the airfields. Eventually, the bombs were kept in underground vaults inside the hardened shelters, thus reducing time spent on loading, and further shortening reaction time.

ABOVE By 1964, the standard British nuclear bomb was the WE177, for delivery by air as a bomb or as a helicopter-launched depth charge. Physically smaller than previous weapons, it was manufactured in three variants: WE177A, with a yield between 0.5 and 10 kilotons; the 450-kiloton WE177B; and the 200-kiloton WE177C. (IWM, MUN 004664)

ABOVE Sectioned WE177A round at Boscombe Down Aviation Collection, near Salisbury. The weapon is 112 inches (2,845 mm) long and weighs 600 pounds (272 kg). A total of 107 examples of the "A" variant were constructed. (Brian Burnell)

ABOVE Road trials of the WE177 using a purpose-designed four-wheeled trailer attached to a Series I Land Rover; 1965, Farnborough. (RAF Museum, Crown Copyright)

BELOW South bomb store at RAF Upper Heyford, one of a number of secure weapons' storage facilities on the site. From 1950, Upper Heyford was home to elements of the USAF Strategic Air Command intercontinental bombing force, consisting of B-36 and B-50 bombers. (Historic England)

BELOW HAS at RAF Honington, with ground equipment annex. Built from reinforced materials with concrete panel doors, the 128 -foot- (39-m-) long HAS was constructed to a standard NATO design, and was designed to protect aircraft on the ground from both conventional and nuclear attack. (Historic England)

# US air-launched nuclear weapons

Since the original "Little Boy" and "Fat Man" weapons of 1945, the USA has developed more than 30 types of free-fall nuclear bomb, with yields ranging from a relatively modest 1 kiloton to a massive 25 megatons, designed to be delivered by long-range strategic bomber aircraft (see Table 7, below).

"Little Boy" and "Fat Man" were both dropped from modified B-29 Superfortress aircraft, but the size and weight of the weapons made them difficult to deploy. By 1947, the B-29 had been superseded by the B-36 Peacemaker and then by the B-50, an intercontinental bomber that was purpose-designed to deliver nuclear weapons. The first jet-powered strategic bomber was the B-47 Stratojet, which appeared in 1950, but it is the turbojet-engined B-52 Stratofortress that is most closely associated with the air-dropped nuclear weapons of the Cold War. Introduced in 1954, the B-52 has already clocked up more than 60 years in service,

## TABLE 7 US NUCLEAR FREE-FALL BOMBS IN SERVICE, 1945–83

| Date in service | Name and/or designation* | Description and warhead | Yield |
|---|---|---|---|
| 1945 | Mk 1 "Little Boy" | Free-fall bomb; uranium fission warhead | 15–16 kilotons |
| 1945 | Mk 3 "Fat Man" Model Y-1561 | Free-fall bomb; plutonium fission warhead | 21 kilotons |
| 1949 | Mk 4 "Fat Man" | Free-fall bomb; fission warhead | 1–31 kilotons |
| 1951 | Mk 6 | Free-fall bomb; fission warhead | 8–160 kilotons |
| 1951 | Mk 8 "Elsie" | Free-fall earth-penetrating weapon; fission warhead | 25–30 kilotons |
| 1952 | Mk 5 | Free-fall bomb; fission warhead | 6–120 kilotons |
| 1952 | Mk 7 | Free-fall bomb; fission warhead | 8–61 kilotons |
| 1953 | Mk 18 "Super Oralloy" | Free-fall bomb; fission warhead | 500 kilotons |
| 1954 | Mk 12 "Brok" | Free-fall bomb; fission warhead | 12–14 kilotons |
| 1954 | Mk 17, EC 17 | Free-fall bomb; thermonuclear fusion enriched-lithium warhead | 10–15 megatons |
| 1954 | Mk 24, EC 24 | Free-fall bomb; thermonuclear fusion enriched-lithium warhead | 10–15 megatons |
| 1954 | Mk 14, EC 14, TX 14 | Free-fall bomb; thermonuclear fusion enriched-lithium warhead | 5–7 megatons |
| 1954 | Mk 16, TX 16 | Free-fall bomb; cryogenic thermonuclear fusion warhead | 6–8 megatons |
| 1955 | Mk 15, TX 15 | Free-fall bomb; thermonuclear fusion warhead, enriched-uranium casing | 1.7–3.8 megatons |
| 1955 | Mk 21 | Free-fall bomb; thermonuclear fusion warhead | 4–4.5 megatons |
| 1956 | Mk 11 | Free-fall earth-penetrating weapon; enriched-uranium fission warhead | 25–30 kilotons |
| 1956 | Mk 36 | Free-fall bomb; thermonuclear fusion warhead | 6–19 megatons |
| 1957 | Mk 39 | Free-fall bomb; thermonuclear fusion warhead | 3–4 megatons |
| 1958 | Mk 105 "Hotpoint" | "Lay-down" parachute-suspended free-fall bomb; fission warhead | 11 kilotons |
| 1958 | Mk 27 | Free-fall bomb; thermonuclear fusion warhead | 2 megatons |
| 1958 | Mk 28 series | Free-fall bomb; thermonuclear fusion warhead | 0.07–1.45 megatons |
| 1960 | Mk 41, B41 | Free-fall bomb; thermonuclear fusion warhead | 25 megatons |
| 1961 | Mk 43, B43 | "Lay-down" parachute-suspended free-fall bomb; thermonuclear fusion warhead | 0.07–1 megaton |
| 1962 | Mk 53, B53 | Free-fall bunker-buster bomb; thermonuclear fusion warhead | 9 megatons |
| 1963 | Mk 57, B57 | Free-fall lightweight bomb/depth bomb; fission warhead | 5–20 kilotons |
| 1968 | B61 | Free-fall or parachute-suspended multipurpose bomb; thermonuclear fusion warhead | 0.3–340 kilotons |
| 1983 | B83 | Free-fall multipurpose bomb; thermonuclear fusion warhead | 1.2 megatons |

* Other designs were developed and assigned sequence numbers but were not necessarily put into production.

# TABLE 8 US AIR-LAUNCHED NUCLEAR WEAPON SYSTEMS IN SERVICE, 1957–90

| Date in service | Name and designation | Warhead | Description | Range | Yield |
|---|---|---|---|---|---|
| **Air-launched guided missiles** | | | | | |
| 1956 | "BOAR" | W7 | Air-to-surface rocket; fission warhead | 7.5 miles (12 km) | 20 kilotons |
| 1957 | "Genie" (AIR-2) | W25 | Air-launched missile; fission warhead | 6 miles (10 km) | 1.5 kilotons |
| 1957 | "Rascal" (GAM-63) | W27 | Air-to-surface ballistic missile; thermonuclear fusion warhead | 100 miles (162 km) | 2 megatons |
| 1959 | "Bullpup" (AGM-12C) | W45 | Air-to-ground missile; fission warhead | 12 miles (20 km) | 1–15 kilotons |
| 1961 | "Falcon" (AIM-26A) | W54 | Air-to-air guided missile; fission warhead | 6 miles (10 km) | 0.25 kilotons |
| 1962 | "Skybolt" (GAM-87) | W59 | Air-launched ballistic missile; thermonuclear fusion warhead | 1,150 miles (1,850 km) | 1 megaton |
| 1972 | SRAM (AGM-69A) | W69 | Air-to-surface short-range missile; fission or thermonuclear fusion warhead | 35–100 miles (56–160 km) | 17–210 kilotons |
| **Air-launched cruise missiles** | | | | | |
| 1960 | "Hound Dog" (AGM-28) | W28 | Air-to-air tactical cruise missile; thermonuclear fusion warhead | 700 miles (1,134 km) | 0.5–4 megatons |
| 1982 | ALCM (AGM-86B)* | W80-1 | Air-launched cruise missile; thermonuclear fusion warhead | 1,500 miles (2,400 km) | 5–150 kilotons |
| 1990 | ACM (AGM-129A) | W80-1 | Advanced air-launched cruise missile; thermonuclear fusion warhead | 2,000 miles (3,250 km) | 5–150 kilotons |

\* AGM-86B cruise missiles remain in US service as of 2016.

**BELOW** The last flight of the USAF B-47 Stratojet bomber, which was retired in 1986. Introduced in 1950, the Stratojet was the world's first jet-powered strategic bomber, and acted as the first line of America's nuclear deterrent. Many were operated from forward bases in Britain and elsewhere. *(US Department of Defense)*

with examples still flying today, and is expected to remain in US service until 2045.

As the weapons became smaller, more aircraft, including many fighters, were also considered to be "nuclear capable." Later US

**RIGHT** Mk 28 thermonuclear bomb being unloaded from USAF Boeing B-52H Stratofortress aircraft during Exercise Global Shield 84. There were 20 versions of the Mk 28, with yields varying between 0.07 and 1.45 megatons. *(US Department of Defense)*

nuclear bombers include the B-58 Hustler, the A-5 Vigilante, the FB-111 Aardvark and the B-2A Spirit stealth bomber.

## Air-launched guided missiles

The first air-to-surface nuclear missile deployed by the USA was the Bureau of Ordnance atomic rocket ("BOAR"), an unguided ballistic stand-off weapon. Developed for the US Navy, and entering service in 1956, the 30.5-inch (775 mm) diameter "BOAR" was armed with a 20-kiloton W7 warhead, and had a range of 7.5 miles (12.1 km). From April 1959, it was superseded by "Bullpup," and all examples had been withdrawn from service by 1963. "Bullpup" was also a stand-off weapon, but had an extended range of 12 miles (20 km), and was armed with a 1–15-kiloton W45 warhead, or 1,000 pounds (454 kg) of conventional explosive. The improved "Bullpup A" was introduced in 1960, with a total of more than 22,000 examples constructed; this was superseded by "Bullpup B," but both types had been withdrawn by 1976.

**ABOVE** "Bullpup B" was a stand-off air-to-surface weapon, with a range of 12 miles (20 km), armed with a 1- to 15-kiloton W45 warhead. *(USAF)*

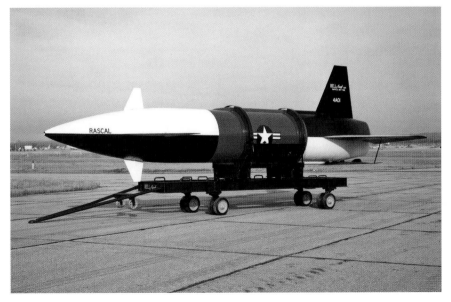

**LEFT** Entering service in 1957, "Rascal" was a strategic missile designed to give otherwise obsolete bombers a stand-off attack capability. With a range of around 100 miles (162 km), the missile was armed with a 2-megaton W27 thermonuclear warhead. *(USAF)*

km). The missile entered service in 1957, with the last example withdrawn just two years later.

In the late 1950s, development work started on "Skybolt," an air-launched ballistic missile capable of delivering a 1-megaton W59 warhead across a range of 1,150 miles (1,860 km). The missile was not successful, and a series of failures during testing led to its cancellation in December 1962. This caused a political storm in Britain as all its other projects had been cancelled in favor of the purchase of "Skybolt," which Britain had planned to deploy in the V-Bomber fleet. Work had already been done on a number of Vulcans to allow "Skybolt" missiles to be carried outboard of the wing landing gear. Britain was eventually offered "Polaris" in its place and the converted Vulcans were modified to accept US "Shrike" air-to-surface missiles designed for use against radar and communications targets.

The short-range attack missile (SRAM) filled the gap left by the cancelled "Skybolt" project, and provided the USAF with an air-to-surface nuclear missile armed with a W69 warhead that had a 17-kiloton yield in fission mode and 210 kilotons in fusion mode. SRAM was the smallest strategic nuclear weapon

**ABOVE Inert SRAM being loaded to a USAF Rockwell B-1B heavy strategic bomber.** *(US Department of Defense)*

Unlike "BOAR," which had been developed for naval use, "Rascal" was a strategic missile designed to give otherwise obsolete bombers a stand-off attack capability. Armed with a 2-megaton W27 thermonuclear warhead, "Rascal" had a range of around 100 miles (160

**BELOW B-52F long-range bomber taking off with its complement of two "Hound Dog" cruise missiles mounted under the wings. "Hound Dog" was introduced in 1959, and carried a W28 thermonuclear warhead with a variable 0.5- to 4-megaton yield.** *(US Department of Defense)*

carried by US aircraft, and 20 missiles could be accommodated in a single B-52 along with four Mk 28 free-fall bombs with a variable 0.07 to 1.45-megaton yield. The operating range was 100 miles (160 km) when fired at high altitude, and 35 miles (56 km) at low altitude. Production began in 1971, with the first examples delivered in March the following year. SRAMs were withdrawn in June 1990.

## Cruise missiles

Originally described as "aerial torpedoes," cruise missiles are fitted with small wings and are designed to travel at a more or less constant velocity, either subsonic or supersonic. The missiles can be launched from air, land, surface ship or submarine, and are generally directed at distant tactical targets on land or at sea. Modern electronic guidance systems provide a high degree of accuracy.

"Hound Dog" was the first cruise weapon to be deployed by a USAF bomber, and was introduced into service in 1959, carrying a W28 thermonuclear warhead with a variable 0.5- to 4-megaton yield. Two "Hound Dogs" could be carried underslung beneath a B-52, giving the aircraft the ability to attack two separate radar installations or surface-to-air missile sites, whilst

remaining out of range. "Hound Dog" continued in service for more than 15 years, with the last example removed from the front line in 1975; a number were retained in the USA's nuclear stockpile until 1978.

Development of the "air-launched cruise missile" (ALCM) began in January 1968; it was originally intended as a decoy weapon that could confuse enemy radar into believing that it was "seeing" a B-52 bomber. By 1973, the project had evolved into a nuclear-armed long-range cruise missile carrying a 200-kiloton W80-1 warhead. A single B-52 bomber was able to carry 20 ALCMs on wing pylons, as well as four Mk 28 bombs. Production began in January 1977, and, by 1980, the original ALCM had been superseded by a larger version with an extended range, although the number of missiles carried by the B-52 was reduced to ten.

The last production example was delivered in October 1986, and ALCM was eventually replaced by the "advanced cruise missile," similarly armed with a W80-1 warhead with a variable yield of 5 to 150 kilotons, but providing greater range and a minimal radar signature. Deliveries began in June 1990, ending in August the following year.

**BELOW** The ALCM entered production in 1977. A single B-52 bomber could carry 20 ALCMs, each with a 200-kiloton W80-1 warhead, as well as four Mk 28 nuclear bombs. (*US Department of Defense*)

*"To make our contribution to the deterrent we must ourselves possess the most up-to-date nuclear weapons, and the means of delivering them."*

**Winston Churchill, speech in the House of Commons, March 1, 1955**

## Chapter Five
# Land-based nuclear weapons

"Little Boy" and "Fat Man" were complex, physically large and relatively heavy weapons, and there was no alternative but to deliver them by air using specially modified aircraft. The size of the weapons meant that it would not have been possible for more than one to be carried, even if more had been available at the time, and land-based delivery across even a short distance was not feasible. Immediately after the end of the Second World War, the USA started to research the miniaturization and standardization of nuclear warheads, in order both to simplify their deployment and to allow the use of alternative delivery methods.

**OPPOSITE** Introduced into service in Europe in 1954, the truck-mounted "Honest John" was the US Army's first nuclear-capable surface-to-surface missile. Examples served with the Royal Artillery between 1959 and 1976. *(Warehouse Collection)*

**ABOVE** Initially equipped with a 1.44-megaton W49 warhead, "Atlas" was the first ICBM, capable of reaching the Soviet Union from bases in the USA. *(US Department of Defense)*

**ABOVE RIGHT** Typical Soviet ballistic missile – the OTR-22 (designated SS-12 by NATO), a short-range rocket with a yield of 500 kilotons, designed to be launched from its **MAZ-543P TEL** vehicle; May 1968. *(Warehouse Collection)*

**RIGHT** Introduced in 1988, towards the end of the Cold War, the Soviet "Topol" RT2-PM (SS-25) ICBM carries a single 800-kiloton warhead. The TEL vehicle is the **MAZ-7917**. *(One Half 3544)*

**RIGHT** Mounted on a modified Bedford RL TEL vehicle, "Blue Water" was equipped with a 10-kiloton warhead based on the American W44, and was a British attempt at producing a viable battlefield nuclear weapon. The project was cancelled in 1964 due to the cost. *(Warehouse Collection)*

By the early 1950s, the USA had developed tactical warheads that could be incorporated in artillery shells and rockets; medium-range missiles soon followed and, by the beginning of the 1960s, the first ground-launched ICBMs started to appear in service in the form of the "Atlas" rocket. Large numbers of different delivery vehicles capable of surface-launching megaton nuclear warheads against both civilian and military targets have subsequently been developed.

Britain, on the other hand, despite having successfully developed independent nuclear warheads and a fleet of bombers capable of visiting apocalypse on the Soviet Union, has been unable to bring any home-grown ground-launched nuclear delivery systems into service, either for the tactical or strategic role. "Blue Streak," for example, was a medium-range ballistic nuclear missile on which work was started in the mid-1950s, but which was terminated before reaching production as being too expensive. Similarly, "Blue Water," a surface-to-surface battlefield nuclear missile – that was also intended for use in the, similarly abandoned, TSR2 strike aircraft – was cancelled in April 1962, before being put into production. From the mid-1950s, the British Army deployed US-designed "Honest John" missiles, followed by "Corporal" and "Lance," all of them armed with

US-controlled nuclear warheads. Britain had also planned to use "Skybolt" before the Americans cancelled it in favor of the submarine-launched "Polaris" and the subsequent "Trident."

## US nuclear artillery

Nuclear artillery allowed the destructive power and deterrent effect of nuclear weapons to be exploited on the battlefield. The development of the first such weapon – dubbed "Atomic Annie" – started in 1949, with the first

**LEFT** **"Blue Streak"** **was an attempt at building a British medium-range ballistic nuclear missile, but the project was cancelled in 1960 as being too expensive. The rocket component was subsequently used as the first stage of the Europa space carrier vehicle, and is seen here on the launch pad at Woomera in 1964.** *(RAF Museum, Crown Copyright)*

**LEFT** **"Atomic Annie" was a 280 mm artillery piece capable of firing a 15-kiloton W9 nuclear projectile across a range of 20 miles (32 km). The size of the weapon was such that it required a pair of specially designed Kenworth tractors to move it from one location to another.** *(Warehouse Collection)*

test carried out in May 1953 at the Nevada Test Site. Officially designated M65, "Atomic Annie" was a 280 mm rifled cannon capable of delivering a 15-kiloton W9 nuclear projectile across a range of 20 miles (32 km); the cannon was 84 feet (25 m) in length, and required a pair of specially designed tractors to move it from one place to another. A total of 20 cannon were produced and were deployed to Europe and Korea, but the system was withdrawn in 1963. Nuclear shells were also produced for the M110 and M115 howitzers, using the lower-yield W33

and W79 warheads, and for the 155 mm M114 and M198 howitzers, in this case deploying the W48 warhead. The nuclear-capable M110 howitzer was also deployed by Heavy Regiments of the Royal Artillery in Germany.

The USA unilaterally withdrew its nuclear artillery shells from service in 1991, and these weapons have generally been superseded by mobile tactical ballistic missiles.

The smallest tactical nuclear weapon developed by the USA was the M28/M29 recoilless spigot gun designed for use against tanks and ground forces. Nicknamed "Davy Crockett" or "the atomic rifle," the gun was designed to fire an M388 projectile carrying a W54-2 nuclear warhead, with a yield between 0.01 and 0.02 kilotons. Production began in 1956, with 2,100 examples constructed; the device remained in service until 1968.

## Nuclear demolition munitions

Atomic demolition munitions (ADM) were "dirty" nuclear weapons developed by the US Army in the first two decades of the Cold War. Designed for use in Europe in the event of Soviet invasion, ADMs would have been deployed by retreating units to destroy roads and bridges, and to contaminate key communication routes, preventing their use by the invading army – a technique known as "area denial." The smallest of the demolition munitions, the special atomic demolition munition (SADM), employing the 1-kiloton version of the W54 warhead, could just about be carried in a backpack, while the largest was armed with a 20-kiloton W7 or W31 warhead. The last weapons of this type were the W45-equipped medium atomic demolition munition (MADM) of 1965, which remained in service or storage until about 1987, and the W54-equipped SADM, which had been dismantled by 1992.

## US tactical nuclear weapons

A s would have been the case with atomic artillery, the use of tactical nuclear missiles would, initially, seem to be self-defeating since the resulting radiation would render areas of the battlefield hazardous for both sides. Nevertheless, in September 1947, the US Navy

Board of Ordnance started the development of what eventually became "Lacrosse," a truck-launched tactical missile designed to supplement conventional field artillery, and capable of carrying either a nuclear or a conventional warhead. The range was just 12 miles (20 km), and the weapon was guided by a forward observation post mounted on a Jeep. Testing began in 1954, but the difficulties encountered meant that the first missile did not enter service until July 1959. In its nuclear-equipped form, "Lacrosse" carried a 10-kiloton W40 boosted-fission warhead. Almost 1,200 examples were constructed, but all had been withdrawn by 1964.

The problems with the "Lacrosse" project meant that the first US-designed surface-to-surface missile to enter service that was actually capable of carrying a nuclear payload was "Honest John." Properly designated "artillery rocket XM31" and later simply "M31," "Honest John" was a fin-stabilized unguided device similar to the German V2 of the Second World War. It was able to deliver either a 20-kiloton W7 warhead, or the later 30-kiloton W31; non-nuclear payloads included 1,500 pounds (682 kg) of conventional explosive, or the M190 chemical cluster warhead carrying M134 or M139 sarin bomblets. The range was just 15 miles (25 km), and the missile was designed to be launched from a truck-mounted ramp. The first example was tested during June 1951, with production of some 7,000 missiles starting in 1952. "Honest John" battalions were deployed in Europe in early 1954, and the missile served with 15 nations, including Britain, Belgium,

**ABOVE** "Honest John" was effectively made obsolete by the introduction of "Corporal," a tactical guided missile capable of carrying either a 20-kiloton W7 warhead or 1,500 pounds (680 kg) of conventional explosive across 87 miles (140 km). The photograph shows a development version of the weapon, together with the smaller "Private" experimental rocket that was used to help develop the concept of fin-stabilization. *(NASA/JPL-Caltech)*

**BELOW** "Corporal" missile on its distinctive transporter-erector (TE) vehicle; once the missile was readied for launch, the vehicle was withdrawn. The Royal Artillery deployed two "Corporal" regiments in West Germany from the mid- to late 1950s. *(Warehouse Collection)*

France and West Germany, with the nuclear warheads under what was described as "two-key" control, meaning that a US authentication officer was always in attendance before launch. The last examples were withdrawn in 1985.

"Honest John" remained in service for 30 years, despite the fact that in 1954 it was rendered obsolete by the development of the "Corporal" short-range tactical missile. Designed by a partnership of the Firestone Tire and Rubber Company, Gilfillan Brothers, the Douglas Aircraft Company and the Jet Propulsion Laboratory at Caltech, "Corporal" was capable of carrying either a 20-kiloton W7 nuclear-fission tactical warhead or 1,500 pounds (680 kg) of conventional explosive across a range of 87 miles (140 km). The use of a ground-based guidance system made it the first example of an American guided weapon, although "Corporal 2" was introduced in 1956 in an attempt to solve problems with the guidance system. The weapon remained in service until 1963, with some 1,100 examples constructed. A number were supplied to Britain from 1956 and were deployed by Guided Weapons Regiments of the Royal Artillery, again with the nuclear warheads under "two-key" control.

A lightweight version of "Honest John" was tested in 1956, under the designation "Little John" and armed with a 10-kiloton W45 warhead. It was the smallest nuclear-capable rocket deployed by the US Army, and two "Little John" rockets could be carried in a standard 6 x 6 truck. The weapon was designed to be launched from a special trailer, and the complete rocket and trailer assembly could be moved to the launch site by Jeep. Few were constructed, however, and the weapon was withdrawn in August 1969.

Designed to supersede "Corporal," "Sergeant" was a short-range, surface-to-surface solid-fuel tactical ballistic missile with an inertia guidance system. The designated warhead was the 200-kiloton W52, developed especially for this application, and the range was between 25 and 85 miles (40–135 km). "Sergeant" entered production in 1962, and was deployed overseas by the next year. By 1972, it was replaced by "Lance," a tactical ballistic missile able to deliver a 100-kiloton W70 nuclear warhead or a conventional high-

**RIGHT** Test firing of the "Sergeant" short-range, surface-to-surface tactical ballistic missile at White Sands in 1961. Carrying a 200-kiloton W52 warhead, "Sergeant" was designed to supersede "Corporal," and had a range of 25 to 85 miles (40–135 km). *(US Department of Defense)*

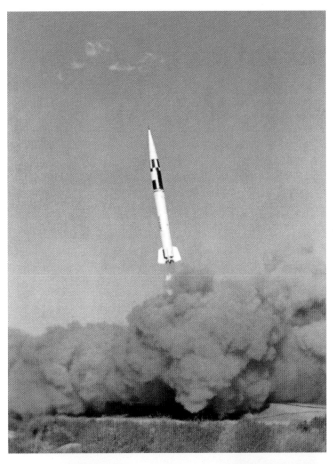

explosive payload. Between 1981 and 1992, the 1-kiloton W70-3 enhanced-radiation warhead was also used, being particularly effective against armored vehicles. "Lance" was the last battlefield nuclear weapon deployed by the US Army, and was also deployed by 50th Missile Regiment, Royal Artillery.

Deployment of the surface-to-air "Nike Hercules" began in 1958, to provide a medium- and high-altitude long-range air-defense weapon for NATO and US forces. Based on the

**BELOW** By 1972, "Sergeant" had been replaced by the 100-kiloton "Lance" missile, seen here being readied for test firing. "Lance" was also deployed by 50th Missile Regiment, Royal Artillery. *(US Department of Defense)*

**BELOW RIGHT** Mounted on the M752 self-propelled mobile launch vehicle, "Lance" was the last battlefield nuclear weapon deployed by the US Army. *(IWM, CT-001210)*

ABOVE Introduced into service in 1952, "Matador" carried a 40–50 kiloton W45 nuclear warhead and was equipped with a radar-directed radio guidance system. It was the first cruise missile to be deployed by the USAF, with 1,200 examples constructed. *(US Department of Defense)*

BELOW Derived from the earlier "Nike" anti-aircraft missile, "Nike-Hercules" was a medium- and high-altitude long-range air-defense weapon carrying a 20-kiloton W31 nuclear warhead; early examples were equipped with a W7 warhead. *(US Department of Defense)*

world's first anti-aircraft missile system, "Nike," which dated from 1953, the two-stage "Nike Hercules" was intended to deliver a 20-kiloton W31 nuclear warhead, although early examples were equipped with a W7 warhead. Nuclear-armed "Nike Hercules" missiles were deployed in the USA, as well as with the Greek, Italian, South Korean and Turkish Armies, under "two-key" control; the missile was also deployed by Belgian, Dutch and US forces in West Germany. It was completely withdrawn by 1988.

## Cruise missiles

Although more generally deployed from aircraft and shipping, ground-launched cruise missiles (GLCM) have been in the US nuclear arsenal since the introduction of the Martin MGM-1 "Matador" in 1952. Carrying a 40–50 kiloton W45 nuclear warhead, "Matador" was similar to the German V1 flying bomb of the Second World War, but was equipped with a radar-directed radio guidance system that allowed course corrections to be made during flight. A total of 1,200 examples were built, the last leaving service in 1962.

Making its first appearance in service in the 1970s, the McDonnell Douglas BGM-109 "Tomahawk" was a ground-launched, all-weather medium- to long-range, low-altitude land-attack cruise missile capable of deploying both conventional and nuclear warheads. The guidance system, used in conjunction with either "inertial and terrain contour matching" radar guidance and optical "digital scene matching area correlation" data, or with GPS satellite navigation and on-board programming, allowed extremely accurate targeting, and its relatively small size made radar detection difficult. The BGM-109A variant, development of which started in 1980, carried a W80 thermonuclear warhead with a yield variable between 5 and 150 kilotons, while the BGM-109G "Gryphon" variant used

LEFT Ground-launched "Tomahawk" cruise missiles were introduced in the 1970s, with a guidance system that allowed precise targeting of individual targets with minimal collateral damage, even through heavily defended airspace. *(Raytheon)*

a W84 warhead, with a yield between 0.2 and 150 kilotons.

In the 1980s, RAF Molesworth and Greenham Common were selected as the British bases for 160 "Gryphon" cruise missiles, leading to nearly a decade of civilian protest. These, and other ground-launched nuclear-armed cruise missiles, were withdrawn from service in 1991 to comply with the Intermediate-Range Nuclear Forces Treaty, but a quantity of W84 warheads remain in storage.

# US strategic nuclear weapons

High-yield strategic nuclear weapons are designed to be used against military targets such as command centers, factories, missile launch sites, and communications and early warning facilities, as well as against towns and cities. Early weapons of this type were deployed from aircraft, but, by the mid-1950s, the use of medium-, and eventually long-range, ballistic missiles had started to become the norm, the first of these in the form of "Snark," a long-range cruise missile with a yield of 4 megatons.

**BELOW** Test firing of a "Gryphon" cruise missile. The missiles were deployed to six locations across Europe, including RAF Molesworth and RAF Greenham Common, where they attracted considerable protest. *(US Department of Defense)*

**LEFT** Test launch of the "Snark," a long-range cruise missile with a yield of 4 megatons. The weapon entered service in 1957. *(US Department of Defense)*

been withdrawn by 1963, as part of a *quid pro quo* agreement with the Soviet Union regarding missiles in Cuba. From 1959, the same W49 warhead was initially fitted to the intercontinental "Atlas," with the range now extended to 9,000 miles (14,500 km); the W49 was eventually superseded by the 3.75-megatons W38.

Development of the "Thor" intermediate-range ballistic missile (IRBM) had started in 1956/57 in response to fears that the Soviet Union was gaining the upper hand in the arms race; with a range of 1,750 miles (2,820 km), "Thor" was more than capable of delivering the 1.44-megaton W49 warhead to the Soviet capital from bases in Britain. By 1958, under the code name Project Emily, "Thor" had become part of an Anglo-American agreement that placed the missiles with RAF Bomber Command at four converted wartime airfields, each with four satellite stations and a deployment of 15 missiles; the first site, at RAF Feltwell in Norfolk, became operational in August 1958. During the Cuban Missile Crisis, 59 of these weapons, at RAF bases at Bardney, Caistor, Coleby Grange, Folkingham, Hemswell and Ludford Magna, were brought to operational readiness, edging the world close to nuclear war. The sites remained active until September 1963, when the missiles were decommissioned and returned to the USA.

**ABOVE** Rocket engine for the "Jupiter" medium-range ballistic missile; developing a thrust of around 150,000 lbf (667 kN) for around three minutes, the Rocketdyne S-3D motor allowed "Jupiter" to deliver its 1.44-megaton W49 warhead across a distance of 1,500 miles (2,400 km). *(Rocketdyne)*

In 1958, the "Jupiter" medium-range missile was introduced, capable of delivering a 1.44-megaton W49 warhead across a distance of 1,500 miles (2,400 km). Some 200 "Jupiter" missiles were constructed, and around a quarter of this number were deployed to bases in Italy and Turkey, but all "Jupiter" missiles had

**RIGHT** In the late 1950s, the USA was concerned that the Soviet Union was winning the arms race. The response was "Thor," an intermediate-range ballistic missile with a range of 1,750 miles (2,820 km), which could deliver its 1.44-megaton W49 warhead to the Soviet capital from bases in Britain. *(USAF)*

**FAR RIGHT** During the Cuban Missile Crisis, in October 1962, 59 "Thor" missiles were prepared for launch at their bases at RAF Bardney, Caistor, Coleby Grange, Folkingham, Hemswell and Ludford Magna. *(USAF)*

ABOVE "Titan 2"in its underground silo with the covers open ready for launch.
(US Department of Defense)

RIGHT "Titan 2" was an ICBM designed to carry a 9-megaton W53 warhead. The photograph was taken during a test launch at Vandenberg Air Force Base. (USAF)

As a possible backup in the event of the "Atlas" project being delayed, the two-stage "Titan 1," an early variant of the rocket used during the "Gemini" space program, was pressed into service between early 1962 and mid-1965, deploying the familiar W38 or W49 warhead. The improved "Titan 2" was a silo-based ICBM designed to carry a 9-megaton W53 warhead, and there were also plans to arm "Titan 2" with a massive 35-megaton warhead, which would have been among the most powerful weapons deployed by the USA. All 350 "Atlas" missiles had been withdrawn by 1965.

"Atlas," "Titan" and "Thor" were eventually all replaced by the silo-based "Minuteman": a three-stage liquid-fuelled rocket with a range of more than 8,000 miles (13,000 km), initially designed to deliver a 1.2-megaton W56 warhead or a 1-megaton W59. Development of "Minuteman" started in the late 1950s, with the first examples entering service in 1962, and the increased range meant that it was no longer necessary for American ballistic missiles to be based in Britain. By 1965, "Minuteman 2" had been introduced, with a 1.2-megaton W56

warhead. The current "Minuteman 3" entered service in 1970/71, carrying a W62 172-kiloton warhead, or up to three 300-kiloton W87 MIRV (multiple independently targetable re-entry vehicle) warheads. "Minuteman 3" was the first ballistic missile to use MIRV warheads, in which each warhead is able to seek a separate target after separation from the parent vehicle, resulting in a greater destructive effect for a given total yield, and reducing the effect of anti-ballistic missile measures. Thousands of missiles had been produced before production ended in December 1978, and at the time of writing (2016) "Minuteman" is the only ICBM in the US nuclear arsenal, with some 450 examples in service.

"Minuteman 3" was to have been superseded by the MIRV-equipped "Peacekeeper," designed to deliver ten W87-equipped re-entry vehicles, each with a yield of 300 kilotons. Some 50 missiles were deployed from 1986, but it was agreed that they would be retired in 2005 as part of the

## TABLE 9
## US NUCLEAR ARTILLERY AND DEMOLITION MUNITIONS IN SERVICE, 1953–65

| Date in service | Name and designation | Warhead | Description | Range (where appropriate) | Yield |
|---|---|---|---|---|---|
| **Nuclear artillery** | | | | | |
| 1953 | – | W9, W19 | 280 mm artillery shell for M65 "Atomic Annie" artillery; fission warhead | 20 miles (30 km) | 15 kilotons |
| 1957 | XM422 | W33 | 203 mm artillery shell for M110 and M115 howitzer; fission warhead | 8.75 miles (14 km) | 1–2 kilotons |
| 1958 | "Davy Crockett" M28, M29 | W54 | Nuclear shells for 120 mm/155 mm recoilless artillery; fission warhead | 1.25–2.5 miles (2–4 km) | 0.01–0.02 kilotons |
| 1963 | M-454 AFAP | W48 | 155 mm artillery shell for M114 or M198 howitzer; fission warhead | 8.75 miles (14 km) | 1–2 kilotons |
| 1981 | M753 | W79-0, W79-1 | 203 mm artillery shell for M115 howitzer; fission warhead | 18 miles (30 km) | 0.1–1.1, 0.8 kilotons |
| **Nuclear demolition munitions** | | | | | |
| 1954 | ADM | W7 | Atomic demolition munition; fission warhead | – | 20 kilotons |
| 1957 | ADM T4 | W9 modified | Atomic demolition munition; fission warhead | – | 15 kilotons |
| 1958 | ADM Mk 31 | W31 | Atomic demolition munition; fission warhead | – | 20 kilotons |
| 1960 | SADM | W54 | Special atomic demolition device; fission warhead | – | 0.01–1 kiloton |
| 1961 | TADM "Sewer Pipe" (XM113) | W30 | Tactical atomic demolition munition; fission warhead | – | 0.3–0.5 kilotons |
| 1964 | SADM Mk 54 | W54 | Special atomic demolition munition; fission warhead | – | 0.01–1 kiloton |
| 1965 | MADM | W45 | Medium atomic demolition munition; fission warhead | – | 1–15 kilotons |

## TABLE 10
## US GROUND-LAUNCHED NUCLEAR WEAPON SYSTEMS IN SERVICE, 1953–86

| Date in service | Name and designation | Warhead | Description | Range | Yield |
|---|---|---|---|---|---|
| **Tactical weapons** | | | | | |
| 1953 | "Honest John" (MGR-1) | W7, W31 | Surface-to-surface ballistic missile; fission or boosted-fission warhead | 5–30 miles (8–48 km) | 2–30 kilotons |
| 1955 | "Corporal" (MGM-5) | W7 | Surface-to-surface ballistic missile; fission warhead | 87 miles (140 km) | 20 kilotons |
| 1958 | "Davy Crockett" M28, M29 | W54 | Recoilless artillery with nuclear shells; fission warhead | 1.25–2.5 miles (2–4 km) | 0.01–0.02 kilotons |
| 1958 | "Nike Hercules" (MIM-14) | W7, W31 | Surface-to-air ballistic missile; fission or boosted-fission warhead | 90 miles (140 km) | 2–28 kilotons |
| 1958 | "Redstone" (PGM-11) | W39 | Field artillery ballistic missile; thermonuclear fusion warhead | 57 miles (92 km) | 3.5 megatons |
| 1959 | "Bomarc" (CIM-10) | W40 | Surface-to-air guided missile; boosted-fission warhead | 248 miles (400 km) | 7–10 kilotons |

| Date in service | Name and designation | Warhead | Description | Range | Yield |
|---|---|---|---|---|---|
| **Tactical weapons (continued)** | | | | | |
| 1959 | "Lacrosse" (MGM-18) | W40 | Surface-to-surface ballistic missile; boosted-fission warhead | 12 miles (20 km) | 10 kilotons |
| 1960 | "Pershing 1," 1A (MGM-31A) | W50 | Field artillery ballistic missile; thermonuclear fusion warhead | 460 miles (745 km) | 400 kilotons |
| 1961 | "Little John" (MGR-3) | W45 | Surface-to-surface ballistic missile; fission warhead | 12 miles (19 km) | 1–10 kilotons |
| 1962 | "Sergeant" (MGM-29A) | W52 | Surface-to-surface ballistic missile; thermonuclear fusion warhead | 85 miles (139 km) | 200 kilotons |
| 1962 | "Terrier" (RIM-2D) | W45 | Surface-to-air ballistic missile; fission warhead | 20 miles (32 km) | 1 kiloton |
| 1970 | "Sprint" | W66 | Anti-ballistic missile; enhanced-radiation thermonuclear fusion warhead | 25 miles (40 km) | 20 kilotons |
| 1973 | "Lance" (MGM-52) | W70, W70-3 | Surface-to-surface ballistic missile; enhanced-radiation thermonuclear fusion warhead | 45–75 miles (73–120 km) | 1–100 kilotons |
| 1975 | "Spartan" (LIM-49A) | W71 | Anti-ballistic missile; thermonuclear fusion warhead | 460 miles (740 km) | 5 megatons |
| 1983 | "Pershing 2" (MGM-31) | W85 | Field artillery ballistic missile; thermonuclear fusion warhead | 1,100 miles (1,800 km) | 5–80 kilotons |
| **Cruise missiles** | | | | | |
| 1954 | "Matador" (MGM-1) | W5 | Surface-to-surface cruise missile; fission warhead | 700 miles (1,135 km) | 40–50 kilotons |
| 1957 | "Snark" (SM-62) | W39 | Surface-to-surface cruise missile; thermonuclear fusion warhead | 6,300 miles (10,200 km) | 4 megatons |
| 1959 | "Mace" (MGM-13, CGM-13) | W28 | Surface-to-surface cruise missile; thermonuclear fusion warhead | 1,400 miles (2,270 km) | 2 megatons |
| 1975 | "Tomahawk" (BGM-109) | W80, W84 | Surface-launched cruise missile; thermonuclear fusion warhead | 1,725 miles (2,775 km) | 0.2–150 kilotons |
| 1983 | "Gryphon" (BGM-109G) | W84 | Surface-launched cruise missile; thermonuclear fusion warhead | 1,500 miles (2,430 km) | 0.2–150 kilotons |
| **Strategic weapons** | | | | | |
| 1958 | "Jupiter" (PGM-19) | W49 | Surface-to-surface medium-range missile; thermonuclear fusion warhead | 1,500 miles (2,400 km) | 1.44 megatons |
| 1959 | "Atlas" (SM-65) | W38, W49 | Surface-to-surface ICBM; thermonuclear fusion warhead | 9,000 miles (14,500 km) | 3.75, 1.44 megatons |
| 1959 | "Thor" Mk 7 (PGM-17) | W49 | Surface-to-surface intermediate-range missile; thermonuclear fusion warhead | 1,750 miles (2,820 km) | 1.44 megatons |
| 1959 | "Titan 1" (HGM-25A, SM-68) | W38, W49 | Surface-to-surface ICBM; thermonuclear fusion warhead | 6,300 miles (10,200 km) | 3.75, 1.44 megatons |
| 1962 | "Minuteman 1" (LGM-30) | W56, W59 | Surface-to-surface ICBM; thermonuclear fusion warhead | 8,000 miles (13,000 km) | 1.2, 1 megatons |
| 1963 | "Titan 2" (LGM-25C) | W53 | Surface-to-surface ICBM; thermonuclear fusion warhead | 9,325 miles (15,000 km) | 9 megatons |
| 1965 | "Minuteman 2" (LGM-30F) | W56 | Surface-to-surface ICBM; thermonuclear fusion warhead | 8,000 miles (13,000 km) | 1.2 megatons |
| 1970 | "Minuteman 3" (LGM-30G) | W62, 3 × W78* | Surface-to-surface ICBM; thermonuclear fusion warhead | 8,000 miles (13,000 km) | 172, 3 × 340 kilotons |
| 1986 | "Peacekeeper" (LGM-118A) | 12 × W87 | Surface-to-surface ICBM; thermonuclear fusion warhead | 8,700 miles (14,000 km) | 12 × 300–475 kilotons |

* From 2007, "Minuteman 3" missiles were retro-fitted with single 475-kiloton W87 warheads from obsolete "Peacekeeper" missiles.

RIGHT Entering
service in 1962,
"Minuteman" replaced
"Atlas," "Titan" and
"Thor," and, with a
range of more than
8,000 miles (13,000
km), it was no
longer necessary for
American missiles to
be based in Britain.
Early examples
were armed with
either a 1.2-megaton
W56 warhead, or a
1-megaton W59. *(US
Department of Defense)*

BELOW It was originally planned that "Minuteman" would be superseded
by "Peacekeeper," armed with up to ten re-entry vehicles, each carrying
a 300-kiloton W87 warhead, as seen here, or a 475-kiloton W87-1/W88
warhead. *(US Department of Defense)*

BELOW RIGHT Test launch of "Peacekeeper" ICBM. Around 50 missiles
were deployed from 1986, but all had been decommissioned by
September 2005 under the START II Strategic Arms Reduction Treaty.
*(US Department of Defense)*

bilateral US–Russian Strategic Arms Reduction
Treaty known as START II. The Treaty was never
ratified, but all "Peacekeeper" missiles had been
decommissioned by September 2005, and,
speaking at a final decommissioning ceremony, Dr.
Ronald M. Sega, Under-Secretary of the Air Force,
credited "Peacekeeper" with helping to end the
Cold War. A number of W87 warheads taken from
decommissioned "Peacekeeper" missiles have
been retro-fitted to "Minuteman 3."

## Missile launch silos

Early missiles were stored in hangars or
underground chambers and were prepared
for launch using hydraulic lifts or ramps. The
underground launch silo, which provides
concealment as well as secure storage and
launch facilities, offers a better solution, and the
first example was designed in Britain in the 1950s
for the "Blue Streak" project. Constructed from
5-foot-(1.5-m-) thick steel-encased reinforced
concrete, with a massive rail-mounted concrete
lid, the silo was designed to withstand a
1-megaton blast, and to protect against electro-
magnetic pulse during launch. The missile was
stored upright in a U-shaped chamber that
allowed the rapid exit of exhaust gas during
the launch phase, and the silo also included
fuel storage tanks at the base, together with six
stories of crew accommodation, control rooms,
workshops and more. A 1:60-scale model was

constructed, and a 1:6-scale mock-up, but, of the 60 silos that were planned, work started on one, at RAF Duxford, and this did not get beyond the making of trial boreholes before the project was abandoned.

The USA's underground storage silos had been used since the introduction of "Atlas" and "Titan 1," but the missiles were stored horizontally, needing to be raised to a vertical position for launch. From about 1963, with the introduction of "Titan 2," the rapid-launch underground silo was developed, so the missile could be fuelled, armed and launched below ground. The silos were sited away from centers of population in Arizona, Colorado, Montana, Nebraska, North and South Dakota and Wyoming.

In 2016, "Minuteman 3" was the USA's only silo-based missile system – housed in the same aging silos that were constructed for "Titan 2."

**THOR IRBM**
**U.K. LAUNCH COMPLEX**

| | | |
|---|---|---|
| 1. LIQUID OXYGEN STORAGE TANK | 10. FUEL VALVE COMPLEX (MISSILE END) | 19. SHORT RANGE ELECTROTHEODOLITE |
| 2. GAS CYLINDER SEMITRAILER (4 PLACES) | 11. FUEL VALVE COMPLEX (TANK END) | 20. MISSILE CHECKOUT STATION |
| 3. LONG RANGE ELECTROTHEODOLITE | 12. FUEL STORAGE TANK | 21. TRAILER-MOUNTED AIR CONDITIONER |
| 4. PANELIZED BUILDING | 13. HYDROPNEUMATIC CONTROLLER | 22. LAUNCHING COUNTDOWN GROUP |
| 5. MAIN TRANSFER LINE (2 PLACES) | 14. HIGH-PRESSURE GAS STORAGE TANK | 23. HYDRAULIC PUMPING UNIT |
| 6. LIQUID OXYGEN OVERFLOW BASIN | 15. RECIPROCATING COMPRESSOR | 24. POWER SWITCHBOARD |
| 7. LIQUID OXYGEN VALVE COMPLEX (MISSILE END) | 16. FUEL FILTER UNIT | 25. LIQUID OXYGEN VALVE COMPLEX (TANK END) |
| 8. REVETMENT (2 PLACES) | 17. PANELIZED BUILDING STANDING WALL | 26. VACUUM PUMP |
| 9. ERECTING-LAUNCHING MOUNT | 18. DOWN RANGE (REFERENCE ONLY) | |

## Chapter Six

# Naval nuclear weapons

Ship-launched nuclear weapons, including undersea missiles, nuclear torpedoes and naval artillery, have been part of the standard nuclear arsenal of both sides since the mid-1950s. The British MoD, for example, has stated that it was "routine practice for Royal Navy vessels to carry nuclear weapons during the 1980s." Naval nuclear weapons came to the fore with the development of SLBM in the 1960s. Constantly on the move, the nuclear submarine is eminently "survivable" as a launch pad, and is virtually immune from attack, making most other types of nuclear weapon obsolete.

OPPOSITE *Vanguard*-class submarine, HMS *Vigilant*, photographed at the Clyde Naval Base. Each of Britain's "Trident"-equipped submarines is capable of carrying up to 16 missiles, with up to 12 nuclear warheads per missile; in 2010, the figure was reduced to 8 operational missiles and a maximum of 40 warheads. *(Ministry of Defence)*

**LEFT** Early "Polaris A1" on the launch pad. Although the first examples were test launched from Cape Canaveral, "Polaris" was designed to be submarine-launched, with the A1 and A2 variants carrying a 600-kiloton W47 thermonuclear warhead across a 1,200-mile (1,900 km) range. *(US Department of Defense)*

Early SLBMs had a relatively short range, necessitating operation from either the North Sea or the Mediterranean in order to reach the Soviet Union, but by the time the multiple-warhead "Polaris A3" appeared in 1964, the type had evolved into a formidable weapon, capable of delivering its three 200-kiloton warheads across more than 2,800 miles (4,500 km). "Polaris," particularly in its improved "A3TK" form, and later "Trident," have provided Britain's major, and eventually only, nuclear deterrent.

# Submarine-launched missiles

In 1960, the first example of "Polaris," a two-stage solid-fuel submarine-launched rocket, described as a "second-strike" weapon, was launched from Cape Canaveral, Florida, with the type entering service in 1961. The improved "Polaris A2" offered a small increase in range, but by the time "Polaris A3" appeared in 1964 the original 1,380-mile (2,235 km) range had been more than doubled. "Polaris A3" carried three 200-kiloton W58 thermonuclear warheads, but the examples that were supplied to Britain in 1962 ("Polaris A3T" and "Polaris A3TK") were equipped with a British-designed fission-fusion-fission development of the W59 warhead known as ET317.

Most examples of "Polaris" had been withdrawn from service by 1980, with the last "Polaris A3" patrol taking place the following year. It was planned that "Polaris" would be superseded by "Poseidon," the first SLBM to be equipped with MIRV. Initial "Poseidon" tests were conducted in August 1968, and the missile entered US service

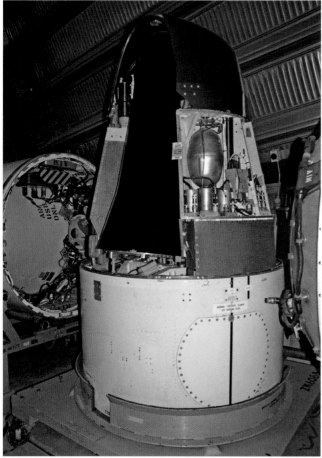

**LEFT** "Polaris" warhead on display at the RAF Cold War Museum, Cosford. *(Warehouse Collection)*

**RIGHT** Royal Navy "Polaris" at Cape Canaveral, **1988.** (US Department of Defense)

in 1971. Subsequent quality-control and reliability problems, coupled with the failure of the missile to achieve its planned 4,000-mile (6,500 km) range were never properly solved and the decision was taken to develop a new extended-range missile, using elements of "Poseidon." This eventually became "Trident."

Meanwhile, towards the end of the 1960s, the British government had initiated a project designed to improve "Polaris" and to extend its life. Using the code name "Super Antelope," and later "Chevaline," the AWRE developed a modified "Polaris" that also released dummy warheads, known as "penetration aids," ensuring enough of the multiple warheads from all of the missiles launched at one time would penetrate the enemy's anti-ballistic missile defense. Unfortunately, these improvements were at the expense of range, meaning that British SSBN (ship, submersible, ballistic, nuclear) submarines would be forced to operate closer to the Soviet Union, making them more vulnerable to countermeasures. However, the project was officially adopted by the government in 1974 and 100 warheads were produced, but, within five years, cost overruns had reached £1 billion ($1.27 billion). The improved "Polaris A3TK" entered service in 1982 equipped with the redesigned multiple warheads, but two years earlier the decision had already been taken to eventually abandon "Chevaline," replacing it with the American "Trident" system.

Work on the development of "Trident," a submarine-launched three-stage ballistic missile with a range in excess of 7,000 miles (11,340 km), had started in 1971, initially described as

**RIGHT** "Trident 2" missile launched from a submerged Royal Navy submarine. "Trident 2" was originally designed to deliver fourteen 100-kiloton W76, or 475-kiloton W88, warheads, but the number of warheads was restricted to eight under the START I Treaty of 1994. (US Department of Defense)

Unarmed "Trident 2" D-5 test launched from the USS *Nevada*.
*(Seaman Benjamin Crossley; US Navy)*

the "undersea long-range missile system," or "extended range Poseidon." The missile was designed to carry up to fourteen 100-kiloton W76, MIRV warheads, allowing US submarines to attack targets anywhere in the world. The system started to enter service in the USA in 1979, with the redesigned "Trident 2" appearing in 1990. "Trident 2" was similarly capable of delivering fourteen 100-kiloton W76 or 475-kiloton W88 warheads, but the number of warheads was restricted to eight under the conditions of the START I Treaty, which came into effect in 1994. Some US "Trident 2" missiles were retro-fitted with W87 single warheads taken from obsolete "Peacekeepers."

In 1980, the British government announced that the Royal Navy would also adopt "Trident," armed with warheads based on the W76 but produced at AWE. A total of 58 "Trident 2" missiles were leased to Britain, with the first submarine patrols taking place in 1994. Since 1998, "Trident" has been the sole British nuclear weapon system, although the question of its eventual replacement in 2028 remains a topic of much discussion. Britain currently has the smallest nuclear arsenal of any of the five nations recognized as nuclear weapons states under the Nuclear Non-Proliferation Treaty, with just 58 missiles drawn from a pool owned by the USA, and is the only one of these states to rely on a single weapons system, described by the MoD as "the minimum effective nuclear deterrent."

## Cruise missiles

The US Navy has deployed both "Regulus" and "Tomahawk" cruise missiles, launched from surface ships and submarines, with both capable of carrying either a conventional or nuclear warhead. "Regulus" was the first US missile to be carried on a submarine, but, unfortunately, required the submarine to surface in order to effect a launch.

"Regulus" was in service between 1955 and 1964, and was armed with either a W5 or W27 warhead, the latter offering a maximum yield of 2 megatons. An improved "Regulus 2" project was cancelled in 1958 in favor of "Polaris." "Tomahawk" started to enter service in 1983, with nuclear variants carrying either the W80 or W84 warhead, each with a maximum

**LEFT** The replacement of the British "Trident" program continues to cause much controversy, although, in fact, it is the "Trident"-equipped submarines that are being considered for replacement rather than the missiles themselves. *(Campaign for Nuclear Disarmament)*

**ABOVE** "Tomahawk" cruise missile being launched from the submarine USS *Florida* in January 2003. "Tomahawk" started to enter service in 1983. *(US Navy)*

**LEFT** Nuclear-equipped variants of the "Tomahawk" cruise missile carry either the W80 or W84 warhead, each with a maximum yield of 150 kilotons. *(US Department of Defense)*

# TABLE 11
## US SHIP- OR SUBMARINE-LAUNCHED NUCLEAR MISSILES IN SERVICE, 1953–91

| Date in service | Name and designation | Warhead | Description | Range | Yield |
|---|---|---|---|---|---|
| **Submarine-launched guided missiles** | | | | | |
| 1960 | "Polaris A1" (UGM-27) | W47 | Submarine-launched ballistic missile; thermonuclear fusion warhead | 1,200 miles (1,900 km) | 600 kilotons |
| 1961 | "Polaris A2" (UGM-27) | W47 | Submarine-launched ballistic missile; thermonuclear fusion warhead | 1,800 miles (2,800 km) | 600 kilotons |
| 1964 | "Polaris A3" (UGM-27) | 3 × W58 | Submarine-launched ballistic missile; thermonuclear fusion warhead | 2,800 miles (4,600 km) | 3 × 200 kilotons |
| 1967 | "Polaris A3T"* | 3 × ET317 | Submarine-launched ballistic missile; thermonuclear fusion warhead | 2,800 miles (4,600 km) | 3 × 200 kilotons |
| 1971 | "Poseidon" (UGM-73) | 10 × W68 | Submarine-launched ballistic missile; thermonuclear fusion warhead | 2,800 miles (4,600 km) | 10 × 40 kilotons |
| 1982 | "Polaris A3TK"** | 2 × ET317 | Submarine-launched ballistic missile; thermonuclear fusion warhead | 2,800 miles (4,600 km) | 2 × 225 kilotons |
| 1979 | "Trident 1" C4 (UGM-96A) | 14 or 8 × W76 | Submarine-launched ballistic missile; thermonuclear fusion warhead | 4,600 miles (7,400 km) | 14 or 8 × 100 kilotons |
| 1990 | "Trident 2" D5 (UGM-133)*** | 14 or 8 × W88, W76 | Submarine-launched ballistic missile; thermonuclear fusion warhead | 4,800 miles (7,840 km) | 14 or 8 × 100, 475 kilotons |
| **Ship- or submarine-launched cruise missiles** | | | | | |
| 1955 | "Regulus 1" (SSM-N8) | W5, W27 | Ship- or submarine-launched cruise missile; fission warhead | 500 miles (810 km) | 40 kilotons, 2 megatons |
| 1975 | "Tomahawk" (BGM-109A) | W80, W84 | Ship-launched surface-to-surface cruise missile; thermonuclear fusion warhead | 1,725 miles (2,775 km) | 5–150 kilotons |
| **Miscellaneous naval nuclear weapons** | | | | | |
| 1955 | "Katie" Mk 23 | W19, W23 | 16-inch naval shell for *Iowa*-class battleships; fission warhead | 23 miles (35 km) | 15–20 kilotons |
| 1955 | "Betty" Mk 90 | W7 | Anti-submarine nuclear depth bomb; fission warhead | – | 32 kilotons |
| 1956 | B57 | W57 | Anti-submarine nuclear depth bomb; fission warhead | – | 5–20 kilotons |
| 1958 | B28 | W28 | Anti-submarine nuclear depth bomb; thermonuclear fusion warhead | – | 0.07–1.45 megatons |
| 1958 | "Lulu" Mk 101 | W34 | Anti-submarine nuclear depth bomb; fission warhead | – | 10 kilotons |
| 1960 | "Talos" (RIM-8D) | W30 | Ship-launched surface-to-air or surface-to-surface missile; fission warhead | 70 miles (112 km) | 5 kilotons |
| 1961 | ASROC (RUR-5A) | W44 | Ship-launched anti-submarine stand-off missile; boosted-fission warhead | 12 miles (19 km) | 10 kilotons |
| 1963 | ASTOR Mk 45 | W34 | Anti-submarine torpedo; fission warhead | 10 miles (16 km) | 10 kilotons |
| 1965 | SUBROC (UUM-44A) | W55 | Underwater-to-underwater missile; thermonuclear fusion warhead | 25–35 miles (40–56 km) | 1.5 kilotons |

\* "Polaris A3T" missiles in Royal Navy service are armed with a British-produced fission-fusion-fission warhead based on the American W59.
\*\* Updated version of Royal Navy "Polaris."
\*\*\* "Trident 2" missiles in Royal Navy service are armed with a British-produced warhead with a selective yield of 0.3, 5–10 or 100 kilotons, based on the American W76.

yield of 150 kilotons. In 1995, a total of 65 "Tomahawk" cruise missiles were supplied to the Royal Navy, although not equipped with nuclear warheads. Withdrawal of nuclear "Tomahawks" started in the early 1990s, with the process completed by 2013.

## Nuclear anti-submarine weapons

Nuclear depth bombs (NDB) are lightweight aerial weapons designed to explode underwater, destroying surface shipping and submarines by a powerful hydraulic shock. Most have a variable yield to allow their use at differing depths, or in positions close to land, and such weapons have been used by the Royal Navy, the US Navy and the Soviet Union. US-built devices include "Betty," a 32-kiloton weapon equipped with the W7 warhead; "Lulu," with a 10-kiloton W34 warhead; the B28 and B57 depth bombs, equipped with W28 and W57 variable-yield warheads, respectively; ASROC, with a W44 10-kiloton warhead; the ASTOR Mk 45 torpedo, using a 10-kiloton W34 warhead; and the stand-off SUBROC, a submarine-launched anti-submarine missile with a W55 warhead giving a yield of 1.5 kilotons. Of these, "Lulu," as well as the B28 and B57 depth bombs, have been deployed by the Royal Navy and by NATO (see Table 11, page 108).

From about 1962 until 1972, the Royal Navy deployed a maximum of 35 "Red Beard" warheads as nuclear depth charges, eventually replacing them with WE177A warheads, delivered by Wasp, Lynx or Wessex helicopters, or dropped from Nimrod maritime patrol aircraft. The WE177 warhead was also fitted to the Australian-designed "Ikara" ship-launched anti-submarine missile in Royal Navy service, in place of the conventional warhead, although there is some doubt as to whether or not any nuclear-armed "Ikara" missiles were actually built.

During the 1982 battle to liberate the Falklands Islands it was reported that seven ships involved in the campaign, including HMS *Sheffield* and HMS *Coventry*, both of which were sunk as a result of enemy action, carried nuclear depth charges with WE177A warheads. The *Guardian* newspaper disclosed that two of the ships, HMS *Hermes*, the Royal

Navy flagship during the campaign, and the aircraft carrier HMS *Invincible*, carried 75% of the Navy's entire stockpile of nuclear depth charges. Despite refusing to comment on these reports for two decades, in 2003 the MoD finally admitted that British ships did possess nuclear weapons in the South Atlantic, but would not confirm which vessels were involved. In a statement, the MoD claimed that it was "routine practice" for British naval ships to carry nuclear weapons during the 1980s, and that there was never any intention to use the weapons, which "were already on board unnamed ships in the taskforce when it sailed." Following the sinking of *Sheffield* and *Coventry*, the weapons were apparently returned to Britain "in the ships with the best-protected magazines."

If true, this put Britain in violation of the Tlatelolco Treaty of 1968 (Treaty for the Prohibition of Nuclear Weapons in Latin America and the Caribbean), which declared that all of South America should remain free of nuclear weapons, specifically banning "the testing, use, manufacture, production or acquisition by any means whatsoever of any nuclear weapons," as

**ABOVE** B28 depth bomb training rounds; the weapon normally carries a variable-yield W28 warhead. *(US Department of Defense)*

**BELOW** In service with the Royal Navy, the Australian-designed "Ikara" ship-launched anti-submarine missile (depth bomb) was modified to accept a WE177 nuclear warhead. *(IWM, MUN-085887A)*

well as prohibiting "the receipt, storage, installation, deployment and any form of possession of any nuclear weapons." Protocol 1 of the Treaty binds overseas countries with territories in the region – including Britain, the USA, France and the Netherlands – to the terms of the Treaty.

All nuclear anti-submarine weapons were supposedly withdrawn from service by the five primary nuclear nations around 1990.

## Resolution-class submarines

**B**y the early 1960s it was clear that the British V-Bombers, armed with free-fall bombs and short-range stand-off missiles, were vulnerable to Soviet anti-aircraft activity and were no longer able to provide an adequate deterrent.

In May 1968, responsibility for providing Britain's nuclear deterrent passed from RAF Bomber Command to the ballistic missile submarines of the Royal Navy Submarine Service, with Britain's first ballistic missile submarine being the nuclear-powered *Resolution* class.

Based on the *Valiant*-class fleet submarine, the hull of the *Resolution* fleet was extended to 425 feet (130 m) to accommodate the missile compartment, with each submarine capable of carrying up to 16 "Polaris A3" missiles arranged in two rows of eight. It was originally planned that there would be five submarines (HMS *Resolution, Repulse, Renown, Revenge* and *Ramilles*), but, in the end, only four were actually constructed, with *Ramilles* cancelled in 1965.

The *Resolution*-class submarines were assigned to NATO, and operated out of a base at Faslane on the west coast of Scotland, with the vessels able to remain at sea undetected for months at a time. The first operational patrol took place on June 15, 1968, and during their near-30 years' service at least one *Resolution*-class submarine was always on patrol in what is still described as Operation Relentless, a "continuous at-sea deterrence" program. During the 1980s, all four *Resolution* submarines were converted to accept the "Polaris A3TK" missile, carrying the British-manufactured "Chevaline" MIRV warhead. *Resolution*-class submarines remained in service beyond the end of the Cold War, finally being replaced by the "Trident"-equipped *Vanguard* class between 1994 and 1996. As the new submarines entered service, the old *Resolution*-class vessels were laid up at Rosyth Naval Dockyard prior to being cut up for scrap.

In 2016, Britain's nuclear deterrent force consisted of four *Vanguard*-class submarines, each originally capable of carrying up to 16 "Trident 2" D-5 ballistic missiles with up to 12 nuclear warheads per missile. This figure was reduced to 8 operational missiles and a maximum of 40 warheads following decisions made in the 2010 "Strategic Defence and Security Review."

**LEFT HMS Repulse photographed in the Firth of Clyde in 1979, with the US Navy deep-sea rescue vehicle DSRV Avalon.** *(US Department of Defense)*

# Clyde Naval Base

Situated just 25 miles (40 km) from Glasgow, on the eastern shore of Gareloch and north of the Firth of Clyde, Her Majesty's Naval Base (HMNB), Clyde, commonly referred to within the service as Faslane, is home to the Royal Navy's *Vanguard*-class nuclear-armed submarines. The location was selected for its easy access to the North Atlantic, and because it was close to the US Navy's SSBN base at Holy Loch, which operated until 1992.

Faslane was constructed as a naval base during the Second World War, when it was described as HMS *Neptune*, and the site became a shipbreaking yard after the war. In 1968, it was expanded to accommodate the "Polaris"-equipped *Resolution*-class submarines, and, in the late 1980s, the north area of the site was enclosed by a high fence, with three jetties and a large ship-lift constructed for the new *Vanguard*-class submarines. The ship-lift can raise the 14,515-ton (13,168-tonne) submerged weight of a *Vanguard* submarine in operational condition completely out of the water. Alongside the missile storage and maintenance facilities, there is a treatment plant for the disposal of nuclear waste from submarine reactors. Faslane has attracted considerable protest from those opposed to nuclear weapons, and has come in for genuine criticism for its safety record, with some 316 "nuclear safety events" reported over a five-year period. During 2013–14, there were six accidents on the site involving nuclear weapons.

The nearby Royal Naval Armaments Depot (RNAD) at Coulport is responsible for processing and maintaining the "Trident" missiles and warheads. Although the missiles are generally returned to the USA for servicing, the warheads must be transported by heavily guarded road convoys to the AWE at Aldermaston. Coulport also includes facilities that enable missiles to be loaded into or removed from the submarines, as well as underground storage facilities for the missiles themselves. In addition to the facilities at Faslane and Coulport, *Vanguard*-class submarines are also repaired, refuelled and refitted at HMNB Devonport, near Plymouth, and, in 2002, a new refitting dock was constructed to support the work.

*Chapter Seven*

# Emergency government facilities

The British government was unable to provide fallout shelters for the population, but when it came to protecting the Establishment it was a different story. From the mid-1950s onwards, expensive concrete bunkers were constructed across the country providing sanctuary from which the Establishment believed it could conduct the war and subsequently direct survivors in rebuilding the nation. There were war headquarters, regional seats of government (RSG), command and communications bunkers, radar installations, county council shelters, local authority shelters, and hardened facilities for water board, electricity and telephone personnel.

**OPPOSITE** Located at the former RAF North Weald, the emergency center for Epping Forest District Council remained in service until the mid-1990s, and was ultimately demolished in 2007. *(Nick Catford)*

The government couldn't dig deep enough, or pour the concrete thick enough, to ensure its own safety should the unthinkable have happened, and many of these subterranean facilities still remain, albeit now abandoned and neglected.

In the USA, some attempts were made to try to protect the civilian population should the worst occur, but, otherwise, it was the same story, with massive underground facilities excavated deep inside mountains for the military and the machinery of state. For example, an underground military center and nuclear shelter was excavated 2,000 feet (650 m) inside Cheyenne Mountain, Colorado. Administration facilities were provided at a series of three-story buildings deep inside Mount Weather, Virginia, to provide an alternate seat of civil government during a nuclear war. For members of the House of Representatives and Senate, a huge underground bunker was constructed beneath the Greenbrier Hotel at White Sulphur Springs, West Virginia, between 1959 and 1962, sufficient to house 1,600 personnel. The facility remained secret until 1992.

## Central government facilities

In times of crisis or heightened tension, the business of central government in Britain would have been moved from Whitehall and Westminster Palace to the emergency government war headquarters (EGWHQ) at Corsham, Wiltshire. The 1962 "Cabinet Office War Book" describes how one of the code words that would have indicated to the Prime Minister that the moment had arrived to evacuate the government from London before a nuclear attack was, apparently, "orangeade."

At Corsham, buried deep beneath a series of disused Bath stone quarries, in part of a former wartime aircraft factory and ammunition store, an underground administrative complex had been constructed with around a million square feet (90,000 m²) of office space. Initially described somewhat prosaically as "Site 3," but later to be known as "Burlington," work had started in 1940 to provide what was intended as a safe location in which to relocate between 4,000 and 7,500 central government personnel, including the Prime Minister, the Cabinet and key civil defense staff in the event of nuclear war. Interestingly, the fate of the royal family seems to remain undocumented.

The bunker was equipped with offices, storerooms, communications facilities, living and sleeping accommodation, kitchens, canteens, a TV studio and medical facilities. Sufficient fuel was available to allow the generators to run for three months, allowing personnel to be supported for a prolonged period, safe from whatever horrors were taking place above ground.

Although the site was far from complete, by 1960 there were facilities for around 1,500 staff. A year later, "Site 3" became officially known as "Burlington," and, by 1962, it is said that the complex was virtually finished, with only the telecommunications system still to be completed. By this time, the emphasis had changed, and "Burlington" had been downgraded to house core government functions, as well as being the headquarters for the War Cabinet and the Chiefs of Staff. By the middle of the decade, "Burlington" had become "Turnstile," with all pretence at having a civil defense function abandoned. Some of the EGWHQ facilities were subsequently overhauled as part of the expansion of the UK Warning and Monitoring Organisations, and a section of the bunker was converted into a nuclear reporting cell. The facilities were upgraded between 1979 and 1982 in order to allow the

**BELOW The so-called "Main Road" in the government's "Burlington" central war headquarters at Spring Quarry, Corsham. Construction work at this former underground aircraft factory started in November 1940. (Nick Catford)**

bunker to operate as a "command nucleus" but, by the beginning of the next decade, the government of the day refused to allocate further funds for upgrading and refurbishment. With just a skeleton maintenance staff, the bunker was kept on standby. Even this proved to be too much and, since 2005 or so, the site has been emptied of its fuel and food supplies and has now been decommissioned.

Since the end of the Cold War, underground facilities for the government have been provided beneath the MoD headquarters in Whitehall. Code-named "Pindar," construction began in 1987. The complex was completed in 1994 and provides accommodation for around 100 politicians, military staff and others, with tunnels said to connect the bunker with Downing Street and the Cabinet Office. Alongside the facilities that one might expect to find in such a building, there are hardened communications links with the permanent joint headquarters at Northwood, and a broadcasting studio that would allow the government to address the survivors of whatever crisis had driven the leaders underground.

## Regional government facilities

Assuming that nuclear warfare with the Soviet Union was inevitable, the Civil Defence Act 1948 divided mainland Britain into 12 regions, each of which would have its own purpose-built war room or bunker; a single room was provided in Northern Ireland. These facilities could remain in contact with the central war room in London as well as with other civil and military establishments during times of crisis. Construction of the facilities began in 1953, with the last completed in 1956, and, aside from those at Newcastle and London, the buildings were designed to a common pattern,

**BELOW** Dating from the early 1950s, and located at the rear of the government offices in Brooklands Avenue, Cambridge war room was a two-story surface building; other similar war rooms were semi-sunken. *(Historic England)*

with access provided via a purpose-built reinforced concrete structure on the surface. The Newcastle war room was constructed in an existing underground bunker (see Table 12, page 117).

In 1956, plans were prepared to construct a system of subregional control centers (SRC) from which rescue operations could be coordinated following an attack, but little actual progress was made.

The development of the thermonuclear hydrogen bomb brought with it the possibility of a change in tactics; a drawn-out war of attrition was far less likely since the enormous power of the hydrogen bomb would allow an attacker to devastate major centers of population in a shorter campaign. If central government were effectively wiped out in such an attack, then control would pass to a series of regional commissioners, each with the power to replace broad functions of the government in his or her region. As before, there were 12 regions, each with its own regional seat of government (RSG) – sometimes described as a joint civil–military headquarters – with some constructed

ABOVE Like the war room at Cambridge, the facility at Cheadle was also a two-story surface design. The building functioned as a SCR until 1968 and later served as the Greater Manchester emergency center. (Nick Catford)

RIGHT Floor plan of a typical two-story war room. (Bill Padden)

BELOW Interior view of Brislington war room; the bunker was abandoned in 1982. (Nick Catford)

1  ventilation shafts
2  map room
3  restaurant
4  tank room
5  WC
6  generator room
7  plant room
8  WC
9  blast-proof door
10 map room
11 blast-proof door

ground floor

0  10  20  30  40  50 FEET

basement

## TABLE 12 LOCATION OF UK WAR ROOMS AND REGIONAL SEATS OF GOVERNMENT

| Region | | Location | |
|--------|--------|----------|----------|
| | | **War room** | **Regional seat of government** |
| RSG 1 | Northern | Newcastle | Catterick |
| RSG 2 | North Eastern | Leeds | York |
| RSG 3 | North Midlands | Nottingham | Nottingham |
| RSG 4 | Eastern | Cambridge | Cambridge |
| RSG 5 | London | Chislehurst; Mill Hill; North Cheam; Southall; Wanstead Flats | Chislehurst; Mill Hill; North Cheam; Southall; Wanstead Flats |
| RSG 6 | Southern | Reading | Warren Row |
| RSG 7 | South Western | Brislington (Bristol) | Salcombe |
| RSG 8 | Wales | Cardiff | Brecon |
| RSG 9 | Midlands | Shirley | Kidderminster |
| RSG 10 | North Western | Cheadle (Manchester) | Preston |
| RSG 11 | Northern Ireland | Belfast | Armagh |
| RSG 12 | South Eastern | Tunbridge Wells | Dover |
| – | Scotland, eastern zone | Kirknewton | Kirknewton |
| – | Scotland, northern zone | Kirknewton | Anstruther |
| – | Scotland, western zone | Kirknewton | East Kilbride |

## TABLE 13 LOCATION OF UK REGIONAL GOVERNMENT HEADQUARTERS

| Region | | Location | Notes |
|--------|--------|----------|-------|
| RGHQ 1 | Scotland, north zone | Anstruther | Former SRHQ and Rotor station |
| | Scotland, north zone | Cultybraggan | Purpose-built, 1990, replaced Anstruther |
| | Scotland, east zone | Kirknewton | Former regional war room |
| | Scotland, west zone | East Kilbride | Former anti-aircraft operations room |
| | Scotland, central zone | Edinburgh | Former Rotor station |
| RGHQ 2.1 | North Eastern | Shipton | Former Rotor station |
| RGHQ 2.2 | | Hexham | Former cold store |
| RGHQ 3.1 | East Midlands | Skendleby | Former Rotor station |
| RGHQ 3.2 | | Loughborough | Former cold store |
| RGHQ 4.1 | Eastern | Bawburgh | Former Rotor station |
| RGHQ 4.2 | | Hertford | Reinforced basement of government building |
| RGHQ 4.2 | | Bedford | Former ROC control center, replaced Hertford |
| RGHQ 5.1 | London | Kelvedon Hatch | Former Rotor station |
| RGHQ 6.1 | Southern | Dover | WW2 tunnels |
| RGHQ 6.1 | | Crowborough | Purpose-built, 1990, replaced Dover |
| RGHQ 6.2 | | Basingstoke | Reinforced basement of government building |
| RGHQ 7.1 | South Western | Bolt Head/Ullenwood | Former SRC |
| RGHQ 7.2 | | Hope Cove | Former Rotor station and SRC |
| RGHQ 7.2 | | Chilmark | Purpose-built, 1988, replaced Ullenwood |
| RGHQ 8.1 | Wales | Llandudno Junction | Former cold store; work abandoned before completion |
| RGHQ 8.1 | | Wrexham | Former ROC control center |
| RGHQ 8.2 | | Brackla Hill | Former underground explosives magazine |
| RGHQ 9.1 | West Midlands | Swynnerton | Former ordnance factory and SRC |
| RGHQ 9.2 | | Drakelow Tunnels | Former underground factory and SRC |
| RGHQ 10.1 | North Western | Goosnargh | Former ROC facility and SRC |
| RGHQ 10.2 | | Hack Green | Former Rotor station |
| RGHQ 11 | Northern Ireland | Belfast | Former regional war room |
| | | Ballymena | Purpose-built, 1990, replaced Belfast |

ABOVE RSG 12 at Brooklands Avenue, Cambridge. *(Historic England)*

BELOW The RSG for eastern Scotland was located at Kirknewton, Midlothian. *(Nick Catford)*

BOTTOM Operations room of RSG 2 at York. *(Historic England)*

at former war room locations. It was obvious that it was all but impossible to provide protection against the blast or heat produced by a thermonuclear weapon, and, although the buildings were of windowless concrete construction, the structure was intended to render protection from fallout rather than blast, so were not bunkers in the accepted sense.

In June 1963, *Hansard* recorded that the role of the commissioner was to "enable succour and relief to be brought to the public after an attack … and to marshal services and supplies for essential survival." This change in approach required a much larger staff, with each commissioner likely to be supported by over 300 people, including 100 military personnel, together with staff from the various ministries, a public information unit, police, fire services, civil defense and communications.

Although supposedly highly confidential, the existence of the RSGs, and their purpose, became common knowledge in February 1963 when members of a group called Spies for Peace broke into the buildings at Warren Row (RSG 6) and removed various documents. Using this material, the group produced a controversial document entitled "Danger! Official Secret," describing the layout of RSG 6, and pointing out that the government had constructed a series of bunkers that would protect, at the most, 5,000 people, and was carefully planning for the inevitability of a nuclear conflict. Between 3,000 and 4,000 copies of the leaflet were sent to selected members of the press and public in time for distribution during the Easter march organized by the CND. As a result of this information, a group broke away from the march and demonstrated outside the buildings at Warren Row. Predictable public outrage followed, but none of the "spies" were ever caught.

From 1962 onwards, the RSG were supplemented by what were described as subregional headquarters (SRHQ), the thinking being that each of the 12 regions would be subdivided into 3 subregions, and each of these allocated a purpose-built fallout bunker large enough to accommodate around 300 staff. By 1966, it was recognized that the RSGs would form a prime target for Soviet missiles and the SRHQs and their subregions were promoted as the highest echelon of regional government

| | | | |
|---|---|---|---|
| 1 | emergency exit | 12 | main entrance |
| 2 | water tanks | 13 | boiler house |
| 3 | kitchen | 14 | plant room and maintenance area |
| 4 | restaurant | 15 | dormitories |
| 5 | switchgear | 16 | communications room |
| 6 | water tanks | 17 | teleprinters |
| 7 | medical room | 18-20 | meeting rooms |
| 8 | sewage pumps | 21 | operations director |
| 9 | telecommunications equipment | 22 | secretaries |
| 10 | regional commissioner | | |
| 11 | storage area | | |

**ABOVE** In 1963, RSG 6 at Warren Row was compromised by a group describing itself as Spies for Peace. The group published details of the installation, including a diagram of the facilities. *(Bill Padden)*

**RIGHT** Floor plan of a typical RSG, in this case based on RSG 4 at Cambridge. *(Bill Padden)*

**BELOW** Floor plan of typical RGHQ, based on the purpose-built facilities of RGHQ 7.2 at Chilmark. *(Bill Padden)*

| | | | | | |
|---|---|---|---|---|---|
| 1 | regional commissioner | 18 | dormitory | 35 | Ministry of Defence |
| 2 | secretaries | 19 | rest room | 36 | army |
| 3 | copier room | 20 | restaurant | 37 | navy |
| 4 | typists | 21 | kitchen | 38 | airforce |
| 5 | office | 22 | ventilation shafts | 39 | typists |
| 6 | meeting room | 23 | WC | 40 | secretaries |
| 7 | deputy commissioner | 24 | shower | 41 | generator room |
| 8 | deputy principal officer | 25 | telecommunications | 42 | plant room |
| 9 | finance office | | equipment | 43 | police and fire services |
| 10 | legal advisor | 26 | telephone switchboard | 44 | meeting room |
| 11 | medical room | 27 | storage area | 45 | Chief Medical Officer |
| 12 | dormitories | 28 | WC | 46 | scientists |
| 13 | radio room | 29 | security | 47 | Home Office |
| 14 | shower | 30 | commander's office | 48 | BBC |
| 15 | WC | 31 | plant room | 49 | government information |
| 16 | recreation room | 32 | WC | | office |
| 17 | offices for government | 33 | teleprinters | 50 | GPO |
| | departments | 34 | tape relay room | | |

| | | | |
|---|---|---|---|
| 1 | emergency exit | | |
| 2 | drivers | | |
| 3 | office | | |
| 4 | dormitories | | |
| 5 | kitchen | 16 | government departments |
| 6 | restaurant | 17 | strongroom |
| 7 | decontamination rooms | 18 | BBC studio |
| 8 | storage area | 19 | telecommunications equipment |
| 9 | entrance | 20 | secretaries |
| 10 | plant room | 21 | MoD |
| 11 | recreation room | 22 | generator room |
| 12 | medical room | 23 | communications room |
| 13 | WC | 24 | WC |
| 14 | dormitories | 25 | government departments |
| 15 | government departments | | |

**ABOVE BBC office facilities at the RGHQ at Ballymena in Northern Ireland (RGHQ 11). Work on the building started in 1987 and was finished by 1990 – as was the Cold War!** *(Nick Catford)*

**RIGHT Floor plan of RGHQ 9.1 at Swynnerton in the West Midlands, a former ordnance factory and SRC.** *(Bill Padden)*

**FAR RIGHT Floor plan of the Somerset County Council emergency center, a purpose-built underground facility close to County Hall, Taunton.** *(Bill Padden)*

government in 1980, with the establishment of 17 regional government headquarters (RGHQ), housed in new underground buildings, or in refurbished SRC facilities. Towards the end of the decade, three new bunkers were constructed at Chilmark, Crowborough and Cultybraggan.

The end of the Cold War brought this particular line of thinking to an end, and the bunkers have subsequently been closed. A number have been demolished, but several have been sold to private buyers to be turned into storage facilities, museums and tourist attractions.

## County and local authority facilities

both during the build-up to, and following, a nuclear conflict. Some of the former RSG buildings were reallocated a role as SRCs.

A new plan emerged following the Home Defence Review undertaken by the UK

In that great British tradition often described as "muddling through," the organization of emergency government and civil defense facilities at the county and local authority levels was fragmented and often heavily reliant on volunteers. A new realism seemed to emerge following the Cuban Missile Crisis of 1962, and the Home Defence Review of 1965 empowered local councils to organize, as best they could, following an attack, before devolving power upwards should the situation eventually stabilize.

Since 1963, county councils had been obliged to provide a protected bunker large

1 entrance
2 dormitory
3 dormitory
4 medical room
5 water tank
6 WC
7 showers
8 WC
9 kitchen
10 restaurant
11 radio room
12 government departments
13 recreation room
14 entrance
15 underground connecting passage

0 10 20 30 40 50 FEET

16 communications officer
17 telephone switchboard
18 telecommunications equipment
19 MoD
20 regional commissioner
21 principal officer
22 WC
23 switchgear
24 exit
25 generator room
26 meeting room
27 information room
28 entrance
29 government departments
30 secretaries
31 registry
32 scientists
33 communications room
34 mezzanine level
35 plant room
36 air outlet duct

0 10 20 30 40 50 m

1 emergency escape route
2 telecommunications equipment
3 controller's office
4 plant room
5 operations room
6 storage area
7 radio room
8 office area
9 WC
10 WC
11 entrance
12 dormitory
13 kitchen
14 entrance
15 decontamination room
16 water tanks
17 ventilation plant
18 generator room
19 diesel tanks

enough to accommodate a staff of up to 80 persons, which could serve as a headquarters during the period of crisis following an attack. The nature of these facilities varied from one authority to another, with some being purpose-built at considerable cost and others, for example, constructed in the basement of the county hall or library. From 1971, county councils were obliged to establish two protected bunkers, with one able to take over from the other if circumstances dictated.

During the last decade of the Cold War, district councils, utilities and nationalized industries were encouraged to construct emergency bunkers to supplement the county structure. In 1987, as part of this scheme, the Home Office was prepared to provide 100% funding for approved bunkers and for other emergency facilities. The end of the Cold War meant that many such bunkers were started but never finished.

## Communications facilities

As part of the post-1948 civil defense program, the government commissioned the General Post Office (GPO), at the time the sole provider of telecommunications throughout most of the country, to develop a hardened trunk-cable network, able to survive anything short of a direct hit. The network was designed to operate alongside the military defense communications network and the government control network, both of which already included hardened telephone exchanges. It would allow the various underground government centers to maintain communication regardless of what unfolded outside, and would connect the major administrative, communications and strategic sites, and handle the data generated by Rotor sites. At the same time, the GPO also established a series of "area war groups" to assist in integrating the various communications systems into a coherent whole following an attack, so that the public telephone network could be made available for military and administrative traffic. A euphemistically described "preference system," installed at all telephone exchanges, would cut off 90–98% of all public telephone subscribers during a crisis, in order to ensure that sufficient capacity remained available for authorized users.

New trunk cables were laid between Glasgow and London, via Manchester and Birmingham, and between London and Bristol, with the latter eventually extended to connect to the transatlantic network. Cables were also rerouted around major cities to reduce their vulnerability in the event of an attack. New "bomb-proof" telephone exchanges were planned, deep underground, in the centers of Birmingham, Bristol, Glasgow, London and Manchester; there was also a government trunk exchange at Corsham. Three of the new exchanges were completed by the end of 1958, although work on those at Glasgow and Bristol was never finished. Three more trunk exchanges were constructed during the 1960s, at Cambridge, Reading and Tunbridge Wells, designed to help handle traffic from London and to increase reliability during time of war.

While the new trunk exchanges in Birmingham, Manchester and London were being constructed, a series of eight hardened "intermediate carrier repeater stations" were incorporated at strategic points on the network, designed to boost the signal strength and counteract losses due to the lengths of copper cable involved. The repeater stations were located at Birmingham (two stations), Bristol, Glasgow, Leeds, Manchester (two stations) and Portsmouth. Built partly underground, these repeater stations were constructed from thick concrete with blast-proof doors, and stand-by generators were installed for use in the event of a failure of the public supply network.

**ABOVE** The London Borough of Lambeth built an 18-room underground bunker into the basement of Pear Tree House on the council's Central Hill Estate. The facility was completed in 1966, but is currently unused. *(Nick Catford)*

ABOVE Exterior view of the hardened telephone exchange at RAF Upper Heyford. *(Historic England)*

By the end of the 1950s, the new hardened exchanges, the repeater stations and trunk cables were becoming redundant due to the development of the GPO microwave system. Although promoted to the public as a means of broadcasting television signals, the microwave system was initially considered to be a vital defense asset which would be largely immune to nuclear attack. Under the code name "Backbone," the system consisted of a chain of 14 stations connecting south-east England to Scotland, designed to provide resilient "line-of-sight" radio-relay connection between key government, military and civil defense locations.

In the mid-1960s, the GPO microwave system was supplemented by a defense-only network connecting all of the military radar stations and supporting the "Linesman" air-defense system.

ABOVE One of three Ruston & Hornsby 500 kVA generator sets installed at the Kingsway underground trunk exchange in London. The generators maintain services in the event of a mains failure. *(Nick Catford)*

RIGHT Typical floor plan for a GPO PR2 protected repeater station. These stations were designed to boost the signal strength of telephone calls, and to counteract losses due to the lengths of copper cable involved. *(Bill Padden)*

BELOW The Guardian underground telephone exchange at George Street, Manchester, was one of five similar facilities constructed in the early 1950s to provide hardened communications in the event of a nuclear war. Taken in 1998, this view shows the 80-inch (2.03 m) diameter cable tunnels. *(Historic England)*

lower floor

| | | |
|---|---|---|
| 1 blast-proof door | 15 transformers | 29 emergency exit |
| 2 emergency escape route | 16 emergency exit | 30 cooling radiators |
| 3 emergency escape route | 17 maintenance area | 31 air inlet shaft |
| 4 diesel tanks | 18 repeater switchgear | 32 generator exhaust |
| 5 generator cooling tank | 19 signal distribution frame | 33 cooling radiators |
| 6 blast-proof doors | 20 switchgear | 34 WC |
| 7 cooling plant | 21 generators | 35 recreation room |
| 8 generators | 22 switchgear | 36 engineer's office |
| 9 switchgear | 23 accumulator room | 37 storage area |
| 10 switchgear | 24 accumulator rooms | 38 workshop |
| 11 repeater switchgear | 25 plant room | 39 blast-proof door |
| 12 cable duct | 26 air supply fans | 40 blast-proof doors |
| 13 blast-proof doors | 27 exhaust fans | 41 entrance |
| 14 switchgear | 28 filtration equipment | 42 hoist |

upper floor

0  10  20  30  40  50  60  70  80  90  100 FEET

## Emergency control trains

It is also worth mentioning special railway rolling stock that each of the British Rail regions held, which were described as "emergency control trains (mobile communications centers)," and intended to allow the government to tap into the telephone network in the event of nuclear war. The Southern Region, for example, had two such trains, consisting of three-coach sets converted from stock that dated back to the 1930s: the carriages were sufficiently narrow to be able to be moved to anywhere on the railway system and remained in service from the early 1960s to the early 1980s.

# Fuel and pipeline systems

I t is an inescapable truth that mechanized warfare, whether on land or in the air, demands virtually limitless availability of fuel. This fact had been well understood by those planning the invasion of Normandy, and, as early as 1942, work had started on the development of a 1,000-mile (1,600 km) long pipeline system, together with relay pumping stations, to connect the refinery and storage facilities at Liverpool and Bristol to a terminal at Shanklin Chine on the Isle of Wight. From here, the first pipeline to France – part of the "pipeline under the ocean" (PLUTO) project – was laid on August 12, 1944, pumping fuel to Cherbourg. Between August 1944 and May 1945, over 172 million gallons (780 million liters) of fuel were pumped to France. Recognizing the importance of the scheme, General Eisenhower is on record as having said that: "second in daring only to the Mulberry Harbours, was PLUTO" for its contribution in winning the war in Europe.

After the war ended, much of the undersea pipework was recovered and scrapped for its metal content. However, the basic infrastructure of underground pipelines, terminals, refineries and pumping stations was retained, together with six coastal fuel depots. In the post-war years, the primary purpose of this system, which came to be described as the Government Pipeline and Storage System (GPSS), was to provide a means of moving aviation fuel around the country, and, during the 1950s, the system was extended to around 1,250 miles (2,000 km) of underground, cross-country pipework,

**ABOVE** As proposed in 1956, the "Backbone" communications system was to comprise a chain of 14 stations connecting south-east England to Scotland, providing "line-of-sight" radio-relay connection between key government, military and civil defense locations. *(Warehouse Collection)*

**LEFT** The route of the government pipeline system is indicated on the surface by white posts with small black-and-yellow striped "roofs." *(Oil and Pipelines Agency)*

RIGHT Map of the
GPSS at the time of
its sale to the Spanish
company CLH in 2015.
*(Bill Padden)*

gallons (45 million liters) of gasoline and diesel
fuel for road vehicles, with around 10% of these
totals used by the military. The same network
of pipes was used for all of the different fuels
and contamination was kept to a minimum by
managing the sequence in which fuels were
despatched: the sequence running from the
lightest (naphtha) to the heaviest (diesel) and
back to the lightest; inflatable spheres were also
used to separate different "parcels" of fuel.

Following a detailed impact assessment, in May
2012, the government announced its intention to
sell the GPSS to the highest bidder. The process
was overseen by investment bankers Rothschild,
with the Spanish company Compañía Logística
de Hidrocarburos (CLH) eventually paying for the
pipeline and 46 related facilities in the spring of
2015; the naval fuel depots were not included in
the sale. A contract drawn up between the MoD
and CLH covered the continued military use of
the system.

## Provisions stores

A nuclear strike on Britain, where something
like 80% of the population live in urban
areas, would have a devastating impact on day-
to-day life and on the maintenance of law and
order. Worse still, Britain imports up to 40% of
the nation's food requirement and a full-scale
nuclear attack would see these imports dry up
immediately as ships turned away from British
ports. Hunger riots would be inevitable.

The government had always assumed that,
for the first few days following an attack, the
population in affected areas would be able to
survive using their own resources. In the widely
discredited Home Office publication "Protect
and Survive," published in 1980, the population
was advised that two weeks' food supply should
be laid-in during the build-up to a nuclear crisis
– although contemporary research showed that
few members of the public seemed to have
any idea how much food was required for a
family to survive for two weeks. There was far
less reliance on domestic cold-storage in the
1950s and '60s, and many more canned goods
were available, but, if the electricity- and fuel-
supply networks were destroyed, anything that
was stored in freezers or refrigerators would
quickly spoil. And, to make matters worse, food

together with ancillary facilities. The route of the
pipework, much of which is buried 6 feet
(1,800 mm) underground, is marked on the
surface by white posts with small black-and-
yellow striped "roofs."

During the late 1950s and '60s, many of the
fuel depots, formerly under RAF control, were
passed to the Ministry of Power, and later to
the MoD. From 1986, the system was operated
by the Oil and Pipelines Agency (OPA) on
behalf of the MoD, working in conjunction with
the Defence Fuels Group. The OPA also had
responsibility for six Royal Navy oil fuel depots.

Eventually, all of the RAF's major airfields,
including those leased to the USAF, for example
at Lakenheath and Mildenhall, were connected.
Private use was also encouraged to assist in
covering the costs of maintaining and operating
the infrastructure, providing it "did not impinge
upon its primary purpose of supplying the
required fuel for defense purposes and did not
require capital investment from public funds." All
of Britain's major civilian airports were supplied
by the system, with something like 40% of
aviation fuel carried by the GPSS. By 2009, the
system was supplying 145 million gallons (660
million liters) of aviation fuel, 58 million gallons
(265 million liters) of marine diesel and 10 million

manufacture would cease until raw materials were available, and until the electricity, gas and water utilities were once again operational. At the same time, the bulk supply chain would almost certainly break down due to the difficulties of moving around the country.

Although the scale of any likely devastation was not of the same order, this situation had already been faced during the Second World War when the government had started building and stocking emergency food stores. By the end of the conflict, there were more than 40 huge cold stores, 16 grain silos and dozens of general-purpose stores strategically placed across the country, generally close to a railway line to aid distribution. Construction of emergency storage facilities continued into the post-war years, and, by 1951, the number of storage depots peaked at 260, falling to 136 by the mid-1960s.

During the 1950s, the Ministry of Food filled these depots and cold stores with a stockpile of 745,000 tons of foodstuffs, consisting mainly of corned beef, biscuits, flour, sugar, yeast, dried milk and other raw materials ready for processing. By the end of the decade, the quantity had fallen to 582,500 tons. However, it was clear that, regardless of how much the government managed to store, food would rapidly become a scarce commodity following a nuclear attack and rationing would become inevitable. On the basis that a starving population was unlikely to be compliant, the government would eventually have to take control of all food supplies, identifying and requisitioning large stocks of basic commodities, including animal feeds and agricultural fertilizers.

The supply of food to the public after an attack would have been administered by the RGHQ, from the bulk stocks held in government storage, from central stocks held in commercial supply warehouses and from food producers and farms, with regard to the need for future agricultural production once any recovery was under way. Emergency powers were available for local controllers to requisition any remaining, undamaged stocks held in shops and commercial warehouses.

However, the Home Office acknowledged that the food stockpiles were, nevertheless, "insufficient to meet the needs of the surviving population over a protracted period," while failing to propose a long-term solution beyond an expressed desire to "re-orientate towards subsistence agriculture growing more food crops, particularly cereal." But the effects of any attack on agriculture would depend, not only on the severity and scope of the attack itself, but also on the time of year. An attack in late autumn would mean that the year's harvest had already been gathered, while an attack in spring would affect vulnerable crops that were still growing. The standard Home Office attack scenario of the period assumed a distributed yield of 200 megatons, and an analysis of the effects of such an attack by the Ministry of Agriculture, Fisheries and Food suggested that 27,000 square miles (70,000 km²) of mainland Britain, some 30% of the total land area, would be seriously affected by radiation to the extent that crop production would be compromised, and agricultural yields would fall by a significant amount. No effective solution was ever proposed, and it seems that partial starvation of survivors would have been the order of the day.

Many of the cold stores were disposed of during the 1970s, and all of the food stocks were sold or destroyed within five years of the end of the Cold War.

**BELOW** Located beside the railway at Haughley, the Stowmarket grain silo was constructed in 1954 and demolished in 2008; the site is now a concrete works. The silo was designed by Eric Bedford of the Ministry of Works; a similar facility was constructed at Ely. *(Historic England)*

# Chapter Eight

# Civil defense

In May 1980, the Home Office published a booklet purporting to instruct the British public on "how to make your home and your family as safe as possible under nuclear attack." Entitled *Protect and Survive*, its foreword explained that the booklet would be distributed free to every household as part of a public information campaign if the country were to be faced by "an immediate threat of nuclear war." For those who preferred to read the advice before such a time, it was available for purchase for 50 pence, equal to about $2.60 (USD) in today's money.

OPPOSITE Public shelters were never built in Britain, but in the USA the government had a somewhat different approach. Constructed in 1961, with a capacity of 1,000, the Highlands Community Fallout Shelter, at Boise, Idaho, was the first prototype community fallout shelter in the USA. *(US Office of Civil Defense)*

"It must be frankly recognised that there is at present no means of providing adequate protection for the people of this country against nuclear attack."
**British Government Defence White Paper, 1957**

**RIGHT** The booklet *Protect and Survive* was published by HMSO in May 1980 and was intended to inform the public on how to protect themselves during a nuclear attack. Highly critical of the government message, the CND produced its own publication entitled *Civil Defence: The Cruellest Confidence Trick*. *(Warehouse Collection)*

**FAR RIGHT** The US government also published information booklets intended to assuage the fears of the public. This example, titled *Survival under Atomic Attack*, dates from 1950. *(Warehouse Collection)*

**RIGHT** List of items for a basic household first-aid kit that appeared in the 1963 HMSO booklet, *Advising the Householder on Protection against Nuclear Attack*. *(Warehouse Collection)*

Two years later, in 1982, Duncan Campbell, a staff writer on *New Statesman* published a blistering exposé of civil defense planning in Britain. Entitled *War Plan UK*, Campbell's book explained that the priority was to protect the government and its ability to continue to fight the war, and, at the same time, to suppress signs of dissent in the population. Following five years' research, and drawing on anonymous inside sources and material that, at the time, were not in the public domain, Campbell suggested that the public was being deceived. He explained that, despite years of often misguided and ineffective planning, waste and misinformation, there were no credible plans for protecting the population, no public shelters had been constructed, and there would be scant medical aid for what would inevitably be hundreds of thousands of injured and dying. The picture that Campbell paints is not a pretty one.

Campbell's bleak and often angry account may not be correct in every detail, but we must assume that it bears a close relation to the truth. Copies of the book can still be found through rare book dealers.

Certainly, much of the advice given in *Protect and Survive*, as well as in a 1963 Her Majesty's Stationary Office (HMSO) civil defense booklet entitled *Advising the Householder on Protection against Nuclear Attack*, borders on the ridiculous. Despite warning that the "explosion of an H-bomb would cause total destruction several miles around," the authors suggested that householders could provide protection for a meaningful period by bricking-up windows, sandbagging the staircase or digging an underground chamber lined with timber.

However, despite a somewhat ambivalent attitude towards the civilian population, perhaps arising out of the scale of the problem, civil defense formed an intrinsic part of the government's Cold War strategy. Much of the planning subsequently proved to be naïve and misguided, or, as in the case of the plan to construct large-scale shelters, simply too expensive, but it did suggest to the population that it might be possible to survive nuclear war. The advent of the hydrogen bomb changed all this. The sheer scale of any likely attack, and the devastating aftermath, made nonsense of any government plans. There was a reluctance to come clean about this, but, by 1968, the Civil Defence Corps had been stood down and the government's civil defense plan could best be described as "stay put," arguing that "no one part of the United Kingdom will be safer than any other." This is true, although, regardless of the reasons in favor of evacuation, there was simply nowhere for the population to go.

If the British government can be accused of failing to plan for the protection of the civilian population in the event of a nuclear attack, it is almost certainly because no amount of planning could possibly mitigate the effects of such an event. Even as late as 1987 the World Health Organization (WHO) was saying that "the plight of survivors would be physically and psychologically appalling." The dishonesty lies in attempts that were made over the years to deceive the public into believing that it might be possible to survive and, even, to rebuild the nation.

## "Four-minute warning"

Since almost the beginning of the Cold War, the idea of the "four-minute warning" has entered into the public consciousness. In practice, it was likely that any warning of impending nuclear attack issued to the public would be of three minutes or less, but whether it was three or four minutes long, the warning was of little practical value. Undeterred, in 1957, the Home Office established the United Kingdom Warning and Monitoring Organisation (UKWMO) to provide the civil and military authorities, and the public, with warning of a likely attack. A UKWMO leaflet boasted that "ten million lives may have been saved" by early

warnings, though it is not clear how or where.

The UKWMO was also tasked with providing details of any subsequent nuclear strikes, together with an assessment of the path and intensity of associated fallout, using a network of 870 monitoring posts across the country. There was conflict between the Home Office and the RAF about who was actually in charge of the warning system, but, regardless, any warning would have been issued by a UKWMO officer located at Strike Command's Operations Centre nuclear bunker at RAF High Wycombe – or elsewhere in the event that circumstances had removed High Wycombe from the equation.

The warning equipment was code-named "Handel," and consisted of speech-broadcast and siren-control systems, linking High Wycombe to about 250 police stations. Construction had started in 1960, and two separate networks were used, routed to avoid likely target areas. If an incoming attack were detected, the operator would press a red button – Cold War buttons always seem to be red – and make a verbal announcement to indicate the nature of the alert. Three levels of warning were defined: "attack warning, red" indicated that an attack was imminent; a "grey" warning indicated that fallout was expected within the hour; and "black," that fallout was expected immediately. The approved announcement for the all-clear was "attack message, white."

High-frequency carrier signals were used to transmit the warning to police stations over the speaking-clock network, and the warnings would also have been sent to the BBC Wartime Broadcasting Service by telephone link. The air-raid sirens were operated automatically, with the familiar rising and falling wail indicating a "red warning," urging the public to seek cover immediately; in Scotland, the warning was apparently to be delivered by "whistle" rather than siren. The "grey" warning, which had been discontinued by the late 1960s, consisted of an interrupted steady tone, whilst the "black" warning consisted of three pyrotechnic maroons fired in quick succession. The all-clear was a steady note.

Under the provisions of the Broadcasting Act 1980, the government assumed the legal right to take editorial control of radio and television channels in the event of a national

**ABOVE** The RGHQ buildings included a BBC office together with a small sound studio from which the regional commissioner could broadcast using local radio transmitters. The photograph shows the studio at the Ballymena RGHQ that replaced the similar Belfast facility in 1990. *(Nick Catford)*

**BELOW** Broadcast facilities at Hack Green RGHQ, now preserved as part of a Cold War museum. *(Warehouse Collection)*

provided in many of the RSG. During the first 12 hours after the attack, the program would have been broadcast every two hours on all radio and TV frequencies set aside for the BBC, and the actual script of the warning has recently been released. It begins: "This is the Wartime Broadcasting Service. This country has been attacked with nuclear weapons. Communications have been severely disrupted, and the number of casualties and the extent of the damage are not yet known. We shall bring you further information as soon as possible. Meanwhile, stay tuned to this wavelength, stay calm and stay in your own homes."

Following the end of the Cold War, the UKWMO was stood down in November 1992.

## Public information

In 1957, HMSO produced its first publication intended to alert the public to the horrors of nuclear warfare, and like most of the similar publications that followed, it was both sketchy and upbeat, not an easy feat bearing in mind the subject matter. Entitled *The Hydrogen Bomb*, the 32-page publication was described as "a comprehensive pamphlet on nuclear weapons and their effects … [including] the facts about the hydrogen bomb." The pamphlet described the nature of a nuclear explosion, as well as detailing the effects of the resulting fireball and blast, and the dangers of radiation. Charming illustrations showed a well-dressed couple with small child, taking refuge under their stairs or in an earth-covered slit trench, and there were the usual platitudes about civil defense and the saving of "millions of lives." Readers who were keen to learn more were directed to the *Manual of Civil Defence: Pamphlet Number 1: Nuclear Weapons*, where the information was considerably more technical and factual. This had replaced a previous publication, dated 1950, entitled *Civil Defence: Manual of Basic Training, Volume II: Atomic Warfare*.

In 1958, taking advice from various relevant bodies, HMSO published a pamphlet for farmers giving information about the effects of radioactive fallout on crops and the land. *Home Defence and the Farmer* purported to "suggest in general terms how livestock and crops could be safeguarded" from radioactive fallout, while

emergency. Television and radio broadcasts, warning of the impending attack and the dangers of fallout, would have been made at regular intervals from the Wartime Broadcasting Service using a special studio at Broadcasting House; fully equipped studios were also broadly sidestepping the government's plans for dealing with the actual consequences of fallout. The publication included, for example, measures to deal with the large numbers of livestock that may sicken or die as a result of radiation, and plans to control the movement of farm produce which may have become dangerous by exposure.

The 1957 pamphlet, *The Hydrogen Bomb*, was updated in 1963, when the government produced *Civil Defence Handbook Number 10*, a 24-page publication entitled *Advising the Householder on Protection against Nuclear Attack*. It was said to have been produced as a training publication for the civil defense, police and fire services, indicating the sort of advice that should be given to the public in "a period of alert." It would have been comforting to learn that "the primary purpose of the government's defence policy is to prevent war," but perhaps not surprising to know that "until general disarmament has been achieved and nuclear weapons brought under international control, there still remains some risk of nuclear attack." There was the usual description of what happens when an H-bomb explodes, together with details of appropriate protective measures,

**LEFT** Dating from 1950, pamphlet number six of the *Civil Defence Manual of Basic Training, Volume II* was entitled *Atomic Warfare* and, according to the Prime Minister's foreword, was intended to "provide all members of the Civil Defence Corps ... with a short manual of practical information about the atomic bomb and its effects." *(Warehouse Collection)*

**BELOW LEFT** A small explanatory leaflet, entitled *The Hydrogen Bomb*, was published by HMSO in 1957 to set out "the facts about the hydrogen bomb"; by 1960, the booklet had been reprinted six times. Those requiring more information were directed to *Civil Defence Pamphlet Number 1*. *(Warehouse Collection)*

**BELOW** Civil defense poster from 1957, providing basic information regarding the hydrogen bomb. *(Warehouse Collection)*

ranging from how to build an outdoor fallout shelter, choosing items for a survival pack and what to do if an air-raid warning actually sounds, including the helpful advice "not to look at the flash" and the notion that taking cover in a ditch might help. Members of the population who found themselves at the wheel of a car when they heard the warning were advised "to park off the road if possible; otherwise alongside the kerb, but not near crossroads or in narrow streets," and those who made it into a bunker were advised to take their birth certificate, marriage certificate, savings bank book and NHS medical card!

Work on preparing *Protect and Survive* started in 1976, and it was published in 1980. Despite claiming that the "booklet would tell you how to make your home and your family as safe as possible under nuclear attack," much of the content was little changed from what had gone before, including the advice to stay at home or to take cover in a ditch. However, more practical advice was included, with the householder instructed on the effects of heat and blast, and warned about fallout. Plans for survival included providing a fallout shelter, building an "inner refuge" for the first 48 hours after the attack, and laying-by sufficient supplies, clothing, first-aid and medical requisites, including aspirin, and other items for a 14-day period. Finally, there was a useful 29-point checklist, but, strangely, since the publication of *Protect and Survive* was supposed to end the secrecy in civil defense, there was actually very little mention of civil defense itself, barring the notion that you should "keep the radio tuned for government advice and instructions."

The CND was highly critical of the message of *Protect and Survive* and produced its own pamphlet entitled *Civil Defence: The Cruellest Confidence Trick*. Although curiously reluctant to defend its own work, the government eventually published a rebuttal to criticism in the 1981 booklet, *Civil Defence: Why We Need It*.

The content of *Protect and Survive* was also covered in a series of 20 animated public information films intended to be broadcast on all television channels if the government determined that nuclear attack was likely within 72 hours. Fortunately this situation never arose, but the films, which were produced by Roger

Taylor Cartoons, were eventually aired by the BBC on *Panorama* in February 1980 in an attempt to highlight the government's woeful record on civil defense planning.

In the USA, there was a more realistic discussion regarding the provision of public shelters, but the authorities were no less untruthful regarding the possibilities of survival. A Federal Defense Administration pamphlet published in 1955 outlined "six steps to survival," suggesting that, with adequate preparation, it would be possible to survive the nuclear holocaust. The writers explained how you could "prepare your family for emergencies," for example by keeping a well-stocked first-aid kit, and sufficient food and water to last a week. Learn how to "duck and cover" if you are caught without warning, memorize the local civil defense signals or keep your radio tuned to the Conelrad (Control of Electromagnetic Radiation) emergency broadcast stations. And finally, follow the simple evacuation procedures and leave the major cities where the threat of blast, radiation and fire was felt to be at its peak – but, better still, build a home shelter!

Retired US Admiral Gene La Rocque, founder of the pro-disarmament Center for Defense Information, was somewhat more honest. Talking to Jonathan Dimbleby on a Yorkshire TV show called *In Evidence*, he summed up the problem with civil defense with these words: "All [it] does is to give the illusion that you can have a nice neat, humane, limited nuclear war. And that's the most dangerous delusion that mankind's ever dreamed up."

## Fallout shelters

In 1946, the Home Office put forward a plan construct nuclear shelters for 11 million key workers. Few politicians could argue with the logic, but almost all disagreed about the high cost of the project. Despite the subject being raised again and again during the early years of the Cold War, nothing was ever done. Even as late as 1980, a plan for a large-scale shelter program was vetoed at a cost exceeding £1,300 a head. The government's view remained that economic realities precluded providing any public shelters.

However, while rejecting any plans to construct public shelters, the government was willing to provide advice to the public regarding the provision of fallout shelters at their own expense. Most of it simply showed how modifications could be made to the home to provide some sort of refuge, and it wasn't until 1981 that serious advice was offered on constructing a nuclear shelter. A Home Office publication, entitled *Domestic Nuclear Shelters: Advice on Domestic Shelters Providing Protection against Nuclear Explosions*, described three basic types of shelter, ranging from a simple garden building cobbled together using readily available materials, short-term improvised structures for indoor or outdoor use, shelters built from do-it-yourself kits and permanent custom-made shelters built into the ground using reinforced concrete. For the latter, the householder was offered the useful piece of advice that "such a shelter might require permission from the local planning and building control authorities." One householder in Norfolk discovered this to his cost when his local authority ordered him to destroy the bunker he had constructed in his back garden; ironically, although it was never fully completed, 30 years later the bunker was awarded "Grade 2 listed status."

The Home Office suggested that householders should not leave their shelter until told that it was safe to do so. Advice from Switzerland, where an extensive network of communal fallout shelters sufficient to house

**LEFT** According to Steuart L. Pittman, the US Assistant Secretary of Defense for Civil Defense, and so-called "father of the fallout shelter," the six points of the iconic fallout shelter sign indicate: shielding from radiation, food and water, trained leadership, medical supplies and aid, communications and radiological monitoring. *(Warehouse Collection)*

**LEFT** Illustration reproduced from the HMSO publication *The Hydrogen Bomb*, showing the understairs space being used to provide protection against flying debris. *(Warehouse Collection)*

**LEFT** Earth-covered slit trench to provide protection against blast and radiation. *(Warehouse Collection)*

**LEFT** Indoor wire-protected steel cage kit shelter to protect against flying debris; dimensions are in millimeters. *(Warehouse Collection)*

**BELOW** Basement window protected against blast by boxes of soil. *(Warehouse Collection)*

ABOVE In Britain, the population was advised that two weeks' food supply should be laid-in during the build-up to a nuclear crisis. Similar advice was offered in the USA, and this housewife was photographed making an inventory of her supplies. *(US National Archives)*

ABOVE In District Heights, Maryland, just 8 miles (13 km) from Washington DC, Harry B. Thomason built this shelter for his wife and five children for just $350. *(US Office of Civil Defense Mobilization)*

BELOW US-designed earth-protected family blast shelter for up to six persons. *(US National Archives)*

INTAKE PIPE

ANTENNA BLOCK

EXHAUST PIPE

BLAST DOOR

5'-4" EARTH COVER

11" ROOF SLAB

EXHAUST VALVE

8'-4"

13'-0"

BLOWER UNIT

8" WALLS

5'-8"

10'-8"

JAN. 1958

**FAMILY BLAST SHELTER (4 TO 6 PERSONS)**

85% of the population was actually constructed, suggested that inhabitants should remain in the shelter for at least two weeks, coming out for an hour at the end of the first week. By the third week, the outside time should have been increased to four hours a day, but the shelter was still to be used for sleeping for several months after the attack.

In the USA, the question of providing fallout shelters was also taken seriously, and American architects were encouraged to cooperate with the civil defense authorities throughout the 1950s and '60s to demonstrate the importance of what was described as "bunker architecture." As in Britain, householders were encouraged to provide their own shelters, either using the basement of a house or building an underground shelter in the yard. From 1958, the US Office of Civil Defense published plans that showed how a home shelter could be constructed. Many large companies and government offices included properly designed underground fallout shelters, and in late 1961, plans were published in *Fortune* magazine showing official proposals for a network of concrete-lined underground fallout shelters throughout the USA, designed to provide refuge for millions of Americans in the event of an attack. Few, if any, were built, but the "other side" seems to have been better prepared, and there are suggestions that the Soviet Union never stopped making preparations for nuclear war and constructed 5,000 shelters in Moscow alone.

## Protective clothing

Designed to provide protection from radioactive fallout, and from some types of radiation, the military "nuclear, biological, chemical" (NBC) suit has become something of a Cold War cliché, conjuring up instant visions of nuclear apocalypse. Back in the 1950s and '60s, such suits were made from impermeable material such as rubber or rubber-coated canvas, and would have included a "gas mask"-style filter. The suit, which was designed to be worn over a soldier's uniform, was intended to offer sufficient protection to allow the wearer to fight while under threat of, or under actual, NBC attack. Until the mid-1980s, the standard British Army protective suit was the "NBC suit, number 1, Mk 3," consisting of a smock, a hood and trousers, with a charcoal-impregnated inner layer. Although not comfortable, the design allowed the user to wear it for several days if necessary.

With the Cold War now firmly in the past, NBC suits – although these days the term is

ABOVE US Army modern NBC suits, complete with mask and gloves. (US Department of Defense)

LEFT Canadian Army NBC suits. (US Department of Defense)

FAR LEFT Decontaminating an armored vehicle. (US Department of Defense)

LEFT British Army Austin Champ being checked for radioactive contamination using "meter, contamination, number 1." The operator is wearing the typical cumbersome NBC suit of the 1950s. (Warehouse Collection)

**RIGHT** The Civil Defence Act 1948 created a (largely volunteer) Civil Defence Corps, and the government worked hard at recruiting members of the public to work alongside servicemen and reservists. *(Warehouse Collection)*

**RIGHT** Civil Defence Corps recruitment advertisement from the 1950s. *(Warehouse Collection)*

**RIGHT** US government poster encouraging members of the public to sign up and train for civil defense work. *(Warehouse Collection)*

generally "nuclear, radiological, biological, chemical" (NRBC) – have become widely available from military surplus shops; but back when they may have been needed, there was little chance of any civilian getting hold of such a thing, and several people were known to have tried to improvise some form of protection. In 1952, one enterprising American devised a lead-lined suit that he believed would provide sufficient protection against radiation. Period photographs demonstrated that this suit was sufficiently lightweight and mobile to allow the wearer to ride a bicycle – whether or not it was any good is another matter.

Notwithstanding the lack of protective suits, the Home Office could always be relied on for practical advice, and *Protect and Survive* suggested that civilians who were forced to take cover after an attack in what might be considered an unprotected building could self-decontaminate by wiping "dust from their skin and clothing at the entrance to the building." Apparently, removing the outer layer of clothing can also remove up to 90% of radioactive material, as can showering in water that is known to be safe.

## Civil Defence Corps

The original Civil Defence Service was established in 1935 in order to provide assistance to non-combatants affected by natural disasters or by enemy military action, most notably as a result of air raids. During the Second World War, almost 2 million personnel, many of whom were not eligible for military service, volunteered for civil defense jobs; including as air-raid wardens, rescue workers, first-aiders, fire watchers and messengers. Both the Auxiliary Fire Service (AFS) and, later, the National Fire Service (NFS) formed part of the Civil Defence Service. The service was disbanded on May 2, 1945, but within three years the Civil Defence Act 1948 reconstituted the AFS and the civil defense functions with effect from November 1, 1949. The newly formed, and largely volunteer, Civil Defence Corps was tasked with taking local control of affected areas in the aftermath of a major national emergency, with the most likely scenario being a nuclear attack by the Soviet Union. Real efforts were made by the government to recruit men and women to the cause, and to convince the public at large that the Corps could provide meaningful defense for the population should a nuclear attack occur.

In May 1952, the Civil Defence Corps was reorganized into two echelons. The first dealt with local issues, while the second, which was described as a "mobile fire column" (MFC), was intended to render assistance to local fire, first-aid and ambulance services overwhelmed by the scale of a disaster. The concept was tested by 600 volunteers from the Army and the RAF embarking on a month-long tour of the country to demonstrate the principle to local authorities. The first MFC depot was opened at Epsom the following year. However, the rate of recruitment was never sufficient and, with the Civil Defence (Armed Forces) Act 1954, the government recognized that it would be necessary to use the armed forces to man the columns, with 10,000 reservists a year, plus at least another 10,000 Army and RAF servicemen, trained for civil defense work. A new Mobile Defence Corps (MDC) was established on April 1, 1955, with a planned 48 battalions, each consisting of three rescue companies, alongside administration, headquarters and transport companies.

The direct involvement of the RAF was ended in 1956, and by early 1958 the number of battalions had been reduced to 40. When National Service ended in 1960 the MDC was disbanded, and the work taken over by Territorial reservists. The run-down continued over the next few years, with the Home Office (and the Scottish Home Department) defining a reduced "light column" in 1963. Further economy measures came in 1967 following a two-year review of expenditure, and the number of personnel was cut back.

In January 1968, an announcement was made in the House of Commons that civil defense would be put on to a "care and maintenance basis," saving the equivalent of millions of dollars between 1968 and 1970. The Civil Defence Corps and the AFS were disbanded on April 1, 1968, and the local authorities were relieved of their civil defense responsibilities. Some 19,000 AFS reservists were told they were no longer required, although the Home Office maintained a register of these personnel for some years. Planning for civil defense continued, but on a much smaller scale, with local authorities tasked with appointing an emergency planning officer. Some local authorities were allocated funds, for example, for emergency feeding plans and for housing those made homeless by civil disaster, but the days of real civil defense were over.

## Role

The post-war *Civil Defence Manual of Basic Training*, first published in 1950 as a series of six pamphlets, gives a good overview of the roles of the service. These include chemical warfare, firefighting, first aid, rescue and protection from high-explosive missiles. Most of these topics, which were intended to "safeguard the civilian population against the effects of war," would have been familiar to veterans of the wartime service, but what was new was the subject of pamphlet number six, entitled *Atomic Warfare*. Unfortunately, there was very little practical advice, and much of the text was concerned with how a nuclear weapon works and what its likely effects might be. After pointing out that most deaths would be caused by flash burns, radioactivity and falling or flying masonry, the manual suggested that an air-burst of a 15-kiloton weapon over a British city with a population density of 45 persons to the acre might result in 50,000 deaths – of course, by the mid-1950s, a 15-kiloton weapon would have been considered tiny – and, anyway, the population density in parts of London, for example, is considerably more than 45 persons per acre.

However, what was clear was the importance of protecting civil defense personnel, who were obliged to work or pass through heavily contaminated areas, from the effects of radiation. Methods of decontaminating clothing and other materials were described, together with a suggestion that different scales of exposure might be required for the public, the civil defense personnel and the emergency rescue services. There was

RIGHT Indicating unit
and connector cable of
"meter, contamination,
number 1." The
meter was designed
to detect gamma
radiation and to
measure dose rates of
up to 10 millirads/hour.
*(Warehouse Collection)*

little agreement on what might constitute a dangerous or lethal radioactive dose.

By the time the pamphlet was reissued in 1956 as *Manual of Civil Defence: Nuclear Weapons*, the science had moved on a bit. The scientific explanations of nuclear weapons were still there, but there was a lot more theoretical information about the biological effects of radiation hazards and detecting and measuring radiation, as well as possible protective and decontamination measures. However, as with much of the literature of the period, the advice that is given – and remember this was a publication produced for civil defense workers – could be described as being "blindingly obvious." Consider these two gems of useful advice: "no-one should be out of doors after a warning of attack has been given," and "after the blast wave has passed there would be ample time before the start of fallout (about half an hour in the case of a large bomb) to enable you to get into a prepared refuge" – although there was no indication of how one might decide whether it was "a large bomb."

Perhaps the fact that the information was still mostly theoretical was an indication of the hopelessness of the task in the face of weapons with yields measured in megatons.

ABOVE Austin Gipsy utility vehicle, widely used by both the Civil Defence Corps and the AFS. Large numbers of these vehicles were released from service showing less than 3,000 miles (5,000 km). *(Warehouse Collection)*

BELOW Trio of Bedford RLHZ "Green Goddess" emergency pump units of the AFS. *(Warehouse Collection)*

## Civil defense vehicle fleet

The MFCs were originally issued with wartime vehicles which had been withdrawn from government storage, often still painted grey, but, from about 1952, a range of new civil defense vehicles started to become available. These included: Land Rover and Austin Gipsy utility vehicles, complete with trailers; Ford Thames stores and rescue vehicles; Commer Q4 general-purpose trucks, hose-layers and pump carriers; and Bedford RL control units, mobile kitchens and self-propelled emergency pumps. Fortunately, the vehicles were never to be used for the purpose for which they were intended, although there were endless exercises and some of the Bedford emergency pumps, forever known as "Green Goddesses," were pressed into service during the firemen's strikes of 1977 and 2002, as well as being used for flood relief in 1994.

When the AFS was stood down in 1968 many of its "physical assets" were placed into long-term storage where they remained for

**ABOVE** With more than 3,000 examples constructed between 1953 and 1956, the "Green Goddess" was well equipped for its civil defense role, carrying a Sigmund FN5 pump with a capacity of 900–1,000 gallons (4,100–4,500 liters) per minute, together with a wide range of rescue equipment. Many of these vehicles remained in Home Office stores until 2005. *(Warehouse Collection)*

**RIGHT** Commer Q4 transportable water unit generally known as the "Bikini" truck. The vehicle held three inflatable rafts and nine lightweight pumps; each raft carried three of the pumps and was designed to allow water to be pumped from inland lakes or rivers that were inaccessible to conventional pumps and appliances. *(Warehouse Collection)*

another 20 years. There was a significant sale of all kinds of kit in April 1989, but many of the Land Rovers, Austin Gipsies and "Green Goddesses," often showing extremely low mileage, were retained at Marchington Camp, near Uttoxeter, where they were maintained and regularly exercised during their long years in storage. They were gradually disposed of over the following years, although several of the "Green Goddesses" were retained until 2005, when the last 900 examples were sold, many with all of the on-board equipment.

**RIGHT** Fordson Thames ET6 civil defense rescue section vehicle. *(Warehouse Collection)*

## Aftermath

At Hiroshima, a single nuclear blast estimated at just 15 kilotons is believed to have killed 70–80,000, with roughly half the deaths occurring within 24 hours of the blast; a further 69,000 were injured, and deaths from the effects of heat flash and radiation continued for many years. The second bomb, with a yield of 21 kilotons, was dropped on Nagasaki, resulting in the deaths of 75,000 people, with a further 75,000 injured. The numbers of people affected, in even a small way, are huge, and, even as late as 1977, more than 350,000 people were still registered as *hibakusha* – meaning they were exposed to the effects of the bombs. By 2014, the number had only fallen to 192,719. Uncertain though they may be, these figures are the only tangible data that is available to estimate the effects of a full-scale nuclear war and, not surprisingly, predictions for the numbers likely to be killed and injured vary wildly (see Table 14, page 141).

In March 1955, a report by Sir William Strath, then head of the Cabinet Office Central War Plans Secretariat and leader of the Strath Committee, laid out a stark assessment of whether Britain could survive a thermonuclear attack from the Soviet Union. Strath postulated that a night attack on the major centers of population using ten 10-megaton fusion weapons would create "utter devastation," killing 12 million people and seriously injuring or disabling a further 4 million: in other words, around one-third of the then population of the country would be affected. Heat and blast would account for the majority of the casualties, causing some 9 million deaths, with less than 3 million killed by radiation.

Strath addressed post-conflict government policy under three headings: life-saving, national survival and national recovery. He pointed out that huge sums of money would be required to save lives – sums of money that were simply not available – and he proposed that an alternative system of government, one not based in the traditional centers, would be required to allow Britain to survive as a nation. The document remained central to the British government's understanding of the effects of a nuclear war on the physical and mental health of the nation, and Strath's assessment served as the basis of civil defense planning in Britain throughout the late 1950s and '60s. The document remained classified until 2002.

Some 25 years after the publication of Strath's report, the British government's Hard Rock scenario of 1979 assumed that the Soviet Union would drop 54 weapons across Britain, amounting to a total yield of 48.5 megatons. This, it was estimated, would result in the deaths of 4 to 6 million. Two years later, Exercise Scrum Half upped the number of bombs to more than 130, suggesting that this would result in the deaths of 7.9 million, while the subsequent Exercise Square Leg predicted 29 million dead. An independent survey later suggested that just a single 20-megaton bomb detonated over a major city such as London would result in the death of almost every living creature within a 5- or 6-mile (8–10 km) radius of the center of the blast – amounting to somewhere around 2 million people. Further out, within a radius of 20 miles (32 km), another million or so would die instantly, or as a result of their injuries. The use of multiple warheads would increase the numbers killed and injured to unimaginable levels: for a major center of population, the prospect of 20 million dead, for example, is perfectly feasible, while being beyond comprehension.

In the USA, there are similarly plenty of scenarios to choose from. The US Congress publication "The Effects of Nuclear War," published in 1979, for example, sets out three possible attack scenarios in considerable detail, while the Joint Inter-Service Group for the Study of All-out Warfare (JIGSAW), conducted studies of the effects of an attack on the USA and Canada, concluding that a Soviet attack on 283 cities, each of which had a population of more than 50,000, would result in the death or serious injury of 81 million people. The study further stated that if the weapons were of 1-megaton yield then an additional 11 million people of the remaining population would have been killed or rendered "ineffective" by fallout; upping the yield to 8 megatons meant that a further 38 million would have been similarly incapacitated. JIGSAW also concluded that an attack on 113 cities in Britain with a population

## TABLE 14 BRITISH GOVERNMENT ESTIMATES OF DEATHS AND INJURIES FOLLOWING NUCLEAR ATTACK

| Source | Date | Number of bombs | Total yield | Predicted casualties | | Mortality rate per megaton |
| --- | --- | --- | --- | --- | --- | --- |
| | | | | Deaths | Injuries | |
| Estimated figures from actual attacks | | | | | | |
| Hiroshima | 1945 | 1 | 15 kilotons | 70–80,000 | 69,000 | 5.3 million (max) |
| Nagasaki | 1945 | 1 | 21 kilotons | 75,000 | 75,000 | 3.57 million |
| Predictions based on war-game scenarios and scientific reports* | | | | | | |
| Hall Report | 1953 | 172 | n/a | 1.38 million | 785,000 | n/a |
| Strath Report | 1955 | 10 | 100 megatons | 12 million | 4 million | 1.2 million |
| Home Defence Review | 1960 | 159 | 477 megatons | 21.5 million | 4 million | 0.45 million |
| Exercise Scrum Half | 1978 | 130 | n/a | 7.9 million | n/a | n/a |
| Exercise Square Leg | 1980 | 131 | 205 megatons | 29 million | 6.4 million | 1.41 million |
| Home Office SAB** standard unclassified attack | 1981 | 179 | 193 megatons | 13 million | n/a | 0.67 million |
| Home Office SAB** classified attack | 1981 | 84 | 180 megatons | 3–4 million | 5–9 million | 0.22 million (max) |
| Exercise Hard Rock | 1982 | 54 | 48.5 megatons | 4–6 million | 5 million | 0.12 million (max) |

* Figures are not available for other exercises such as Inside Right (1975) and Wintex-Cimex (1983).
** Scientific Advisory Branch.

of more than 50,000 would cause the deaths of 90% of the population, while a single 1-megaton airburst over the city of Birmingham would result in the city simply ceasing to exist.

And, the insane logic of MAD says that equal numbers would be killed in the inevitable counter-attack, with similar scenarios and calculations existing for attacks by the West on the Soviet Union and China.

However, although the numbers of killed and injured would be substantial, no one can say for certain what might occur, and, thus, what the casualty toll might be. It is interesting that an extrapolation of the total number of persons killed and injured at Hiroshima and Nagasaki on the basis of a 1-megaton yield far exceeds post-war government estimates for attacks using larger weapons, perhaps indicating a law of diminishing returns (see Table 14, page 141).

## Death and injury

The three major physical effects associated with the use of nuclear weapons are blast and shock, thermal radiation and nuclear radiation, all of which have the potential to kill. By far the greatest number of casualties result from heat and blast, and an analysis of death and injury following the attacks on Hiroshima and Nagasaki showed that 45% were the result of burns, with 50% arising from mechanical injury due to blast. The remainder were the result of radiation, but many casualties were said to have suffered from two or more of the effects, with some 34% being affected by nuclear radiation as a complicating factor. However, there is no doubt that millions would die during the decades following a large nuclear attack.

The radiant energy of a nuclear explosion is released in microseconds with a colossal blast of energy covering the entire range of the spectrum. An enormous flash of infrared heat is emitted for some 20 or 30 seconds following the explosion, expanding into the surrounding atmosphere. The maximum size of the fireball and the period of time for which it persists will depend upon the power of the weapon. For those close to the center of the explosion, this radiant heat, which, it has been claimed, can instantaneously vaporize tissue, will be immediately fatal. Looking at the fireball, even from a distance, causes blindness. It has been

estimated that, for a maximum 50-megaton yield, everything within a radius of about 1¼ miles (2 km) will be instantly set on fire; at a distance of 2 to 3 miles (3–5 km), the human body will sustain second-degree burns; beyond this, the injuries will resemble serious sunburn.

Blast injuries will be the direct result of the overpressure caused by the explosion, or, far more likely, will be "secondary" injuries caused by falling buildings, flying masonry and glass fragments, or overturned, and even airborne, vehicles. The US Atomic Energy Commission's 1962 publication entitled *The Effects of Nuclear Weapons* pointed out that, "for a given over-pressure, a nuclear device is more effective in producing direct blast injuries than a conventional high-explosive weapon because the human body is more sensitive to the duration of the pressure, and this is relatively long in a nuclear weapon." However, the human body is surprisingly resilient, and other publications have suggested that it would still require an overpressure in the order of 45–55 lbf/in² (3–3.8 kgf/cm²) to produce 50% fatalities, with an increase to 55–65 lbf/in² (3.8–4.6 kgf/cm²) causing certain death. In contrast, the typical British domestic building would be irreparably damaged by an overpressure of just 6 lbf/in² (0.4 kgf/cm²), reinforcing the view that fatalities among those close to the center of the explosion are more likely to be caused by heat flash or exposure to gamma radiation than to blast. But for those who might have survived the initial effects of a nuclear weapon, radiation would present the greatest long-term hazard.

The explosion produces some 90 different isotopes as a result of the fusion or fission of the fuel load, with neutrons, gamma rays and X-rays produced instantaneously during the explosion and over a period of time as the products of the explosion decay. The initial radioactivity declines sharply, but alpha and beta particles are also produced during the process of decay. In a ground-burst, residual radiation also results from materials that have been vaporized in the initial blast and carried into the upper atmosphere as part of the fireball, before being irradiated and falling back to earth as radioactive fallout, and as so-called "black rain" containing radioactive soot and dust.

Alpha and beta particles are the most

damaging, but have a short range. Neutrons have a greater penetrating power, but have a shorter range than gamma rays. These effects can be described as "external radiation." Particles of radioactive material will also affect crops, food stocks and drinking water, and will inevitably be swallowed, inhaled or admitted to the body via open wounds. This is "internal radiation." To quote the War Office *Nuclear Handbook*, "nuclear radiations never have a beneficial effect on body tissue," and, when neutrons and gamma rays penetrate the human body they cause cellular damage, affecting the organs and major systems, and reacting with bone marrow. The effects of general exposure to radiation, which are typically described as "radiation sickness," can begin within one or two hours of exposure, and, according to the level of exposure, which is measured in roentgens, or more recently in rads or rems, can result in death in less than two days.

A whole body dose of 350–550 roentgens received over a short period gives a 50% chance of survival – putting this into perspective, the average background radiation level is generally less than 1 roentgen per year, and the Home Office has predicted dose rates in the order of thousands of roentgens per hour in areas of "heavy fallout." Even at low levels of exposure, the sickness may last for several months, increasing the probability of developing other diseases, including various types of cancer.

## Nuclear winter

The phenomenon described as "nuclear winter" comes from climate models which suggest that firestorms following a nuclear exchange would inject sufficient soot and small particles into the stratosphere to partially block the sun. This would result in an "anti-greenhouse effect," lowering the surface temperature on earth for perhaps two or three years, seriously affecting the production of crops. Worse still, in the period immediately following a "nuclear winter," there may be a destructive greenhouse effect that will allow harmful ultraviolet rays to penetrate to the earth's surface, resulting in an equally destructive "nuclear summer."

## Damage to property

The use of nuclear weapons will also cause colossal destruction of property, as the pressure created by the blast damages and destroys buildings that lie in its path. At the outer distance, this damage may be limited to broken doors and windows and damaged roof tiles but, closer to the center of the explosion, the fluctuations of the shock wave will cause buildings to literally explode as the pressure goes first in one direction and then reverses. Fires will be spontaneously ignited by the heat wave. Vehicles will be crushed by the blast, and blown over by the blast wind, and trees will be uprooted.

All of these phenomena will hamper subsequent rescue attempts, with roads in built-up areas particularly blocked by fallen buildings and other debris.

## Law and order

During the wartime Blitz, the inhabitants of British cities that were under aerial attack generally behaved in an orderly fashion, and the attacks were often credited with creating a feeling of solidarity and a determination not to be beaten. However, when faced with death and destruction on the megaton scale of a nuclear exchange, this stoic attitude might not reappear. Even a limited nuclear exchange would almost certainly result in panic in the civilian population, with a rapid social disintegration, and collapse of both the rule of law and the monetary economy. Subversive views would inevitably emerge, criticizing the actions of the government, and the competence and credibility of all forms of authority would continually be called into question. In the interests of maintaining its hold on society, the government would be forced to deal with such views.

A government publication entitled *Briefing Material for Wartime Controllers* stated that "the maintenance of public order would be one of the essential tasks of wartime regional government"; the document described a simplified judicial system lacking the possibility of appeal against sentences. Summary execution by firing squad was also sanctioned in certain circumstances: this being justified on the basis that "penalties such as probation, fines or imprisonment would no longer be effective in dealing with anti-social offenders."

Features of martial law would include measures to prevent the movement of the population, and specifically to prevent any exodus of refugees out of the major urban areas. Special measures would be introduced to detain or restrict the movement of those with potentially subversive views, and MI5 was said to have held a list of 20,000 such people in the 1970s. There were also suggestions that other sectors of the population would have been interned, with military camps made into makeshift prisons. Key routes would be reserved for the military and civil defense services, with the police and military undertaking convoy-control duties. The public would be denied access to fuel, and food stocks would be requisitioned by the government, with feeding centers established and strictly monitored. The availability of weapons would be strictly controlled.

While the government might argue that all of these measures were essential to maintain law and order and to prevent panic for the good of the entire population, there is an alternative view. The stated overall aim of the UK Commanders-in-Chief Committee, a body that was established in 1950 by the MoD Joint Planning Staff, was "to defend the United Kingdom so that it can remain a main offensive base for as long as possible, and an advanced air base in all circumstances."

So much for the needs and wishes of the civilian population!

## Recovery

In his 1955 report, Sir William Strath pointed out that, following an attack by the Soviet Union, the nation's roads, railways and bridges would be severely damaged, and power, water and sewage-disposal utilities would be compromised. The manufacturing base would have been destroyed, logistics and distribution systems would have collapsed. Food and water supplies would almost certainly be contaminated. Recovery would be extraordinarily difficult and would require the government to have prepared detailed plans in advance, and to have laid down huge stocks of food and medical supplies.

Strath identified a critical period following any attack in which surviving segments of the population would be struggling "against

disease, starvation and [the] unimaginable psychological effects of nuclear bombardment." The report concluded that "the country would be left with sufficient resources for a slow recovery," providing the population could get through this critical period, but Strath was unable, or unwilling, to state categorically that there would be such a recovery. There was a small glimmer of hope in his notion that "the standard of living of the reduced population, although substantially lower than at present, would still be well above that of the greater part of the world." But, the road back to pre-war normality would be slow and extremely demanding – regardless of who had prevailed.

## Ban the bomb!

Disquiet about the use of atomic weapons at Hiroshima and Nagasaki started almost immediately after the attacks. Albert Einstein, who had played a small role in the development of the bomb and who had encouraged Roosevelt to continue to fund the work, talked of the "complex guilt" of many of the scientists who had contributed to the project. Popular attitudes to the bomb began to harden, particularly on the political left, and, in 1946, George Orwell, an outspoken supporter of democratic socialism, wrote a highly critical piece for the *Tribune* arguing that "ages in which the dominant weapon is expensive or difficult to make will tend to be ages of despotism," and that "the atomic bomb may rob the exploited classes and peoples of all power to revolt." Even Robert Oppenheimer, generally credited with being the "father of the bomb," had become increasingly nervous about the work he was being asked to do – to the extent that, eventually, he had his security clearance withdrawn.

Yet, despite the terrifying scale of potential destruction available, neither side felt that they had gained sufficient advantage, and, for much of the Cold War period, the situation remained, effectively, a stand-off. There were gestures towards some degree of nuclear disarmament in May 1955 when the Soviet Union proposed that the (then) three nuclear powers destroy three-quarters of their existing weapon stocks, but by September talks aimed at agreeing the

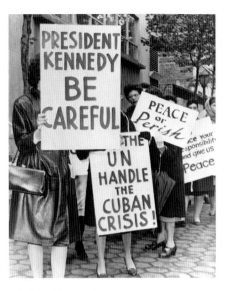

details had broken down.

It was clear, however, that many members of the world's population were unhappy about living with the continual threat of nuclear warfare and, as atmospheric testing became almost commonplace, anti-war movements

began to emerge across the world. In Europe, organizations such as the British Peace Committee and the Direct Action Committee (DAC) Against Nuclear War started to organize protest rallies. The CND was launched at a public meeting in London in February 1958, and, although often associated with left-wing politics, it appealed to all sectors of society, including prominent scientists, academics, religious leaders, journalists, writers, actors and musicians. Advocating a policy of unilateral nuclear disarmament for Britain, the first visible CND action was its support of the DAC Easter 1958 march from London to Aldermaston; from 1959, the march was organized by CND, with marchers walking from Aldermaston to London. By the following year some 100,000 people were involved.

The marches continued until 1963 when the international Test-Ban Treaty was signed. Support for CND waned in response to a perceived reduction in the threat of nuclear war, but the marches were revived in the early 1970s and '80s, the latter in response to Margaret Thatcher's agreement in 1979 to allow US cruise missiles to be stationed on British soil. At the forefront of this revitalized movement were the Greenham Common Women's Peace Camp and the Molesworth People's Peace Camp, the latter attracting both men and women. Both became part of a network opposing NATO plans to deploy GLCM and "Pershing 2" intercontinental ballistic missiles in Europe.

The peace camp at Greenham Common was established in September 1981 when 36 women from a Cardiff-based group called Women for Life on Earth chained themselves to the fence surrounding the base. The protests continued, generating huge media attention – one BBC TV news program actually suggested that anyone approaching the bunkers in which the missiles were stored would be shot! In April 1983, about 70,000 women formed a 14-mile (23 km) human chain from Greenham to Aldermaston and AWE Burghfield where nuclear weapons were made, and, at the end of the year, 50,000 women encircled the base. Although the last missiles left Greenham Common in 1991, the camp remained active for 19 years and was not disbanded until 2000.

By the time the cruise missiles were delivered

to Greenham Common and Molesworth in 1983, another protest group had emerged, calling itself Cruise Watch. So successful was this group in tracking and harassing the missile convoys whenever they carried out exercises on public roads that the authorities eventually resorted to moving the missiles only at night and under police escort.

"Ban the Bomb" protests were not confined to Britain and Europe. Greenpeace had its origins in attempts to stop the USA from testing at Amchitka, Alaska, in 1971, funding the action through a free concert. The US anti-nuclear movement probably reached its peak in the 1980s, with the actions of the Plowshares Group drawing particular attention. A Plowshares rally in Central Park in 1982 is said to have attracted almost a million protestors, while more recently, in 2012, three activists broke into the nuclear weapons facility at Oak Ridge National Laboratory, causing a temporary shut-down.

The CND continues its work to the present day, with the focus currently on protest against the replacement of "Trident," opposition to a nuclear-armed NATO and campaigning for a global ban on nuclear weapons.

**ABOVE** View of the administration building at RAF Greenham Common, containing the missile command center from which the launch codes for the cruise missiles would have been broadcast. Greenham Common was home to 96 missiles stored on mobile launcher vehicles. *(Nick Catford)*

**BELOW** Aerial view of RAF Molesworth showing the protected bunkers in which the cruise missiles were stored. Each bunker consisted of three bays, each housing one MAN tractor, one BGM-109G ground-launched cruise missile TEL semi-trailer and 16 missiles; there were also two launch control centers. *(US Department of Defense)*

*"Now is the time to affirm not only the immorality of nuclear weapons but the immorality of their possession, thereby clearing the road to abolition."*

**Pope Francis, December 2014**

# Epilogue

For 70 years the world has teetered on the nuclear precipice, sometimes coming close to catastrophe, at other times taking a step or two back. Nevertheless, nuclear weapons remain a part of life.

Perhaps it is the fact that the opposing ideologies face one another with equivalent firepower that has helped to maintain peace, but many would argue it is inevitable that, someday, someone will "press the button" that unleashes a Third World War. No one knows how such an exchange might occur or how long it might last, or how many nuclear weapons might be deployed. And no one knows whether there would be any warning.

Any world leader who considers that using nuclear weapons is a legitimate form of warfare would almost certainly be guilty of genocide and war crimes. However, if the politicians, military brass, civil servants and local authority apparatchiks take to the bunkers, then, regardless of any notions of who might "win" the war, the real question is who will be available to do the menial work when the survivors emerge blinking in the weak sunlight of nuclear winter? The impact of even a limited nuclear attack would be devastating. Who will be available to tend the sick and bury the millions of dead? Who will mend the roads, restore the water and supplies, clear the rubble? How will law and order be restored among the angry, disillusioned and frightened survivors, and who will house and feed them?

Despite the unimaginable scale of the slaughter, millions will be unfortunate enough to survive. Conditions immediately after an attack will become worse before they started to get better, and what remains of the nation will be weaker in every sense. The government might choose to suggest that "civil defense" is the answer and that some sort of meaningful recovery is possible, but many natural resources will have been destroyed, together with huge parts of the infrastructure. Large regions of the country will be rendered uninhabitable, whether through the results of radiation, spreading disease, massive damage, or a complete breakdown in law and order, and life will be extremely hard, unpleasant and dangerous – probably for years following the attack.

## Nuclear accidents

Ironically, many believe that a Third World War will be the result of nuclear accident or misunderstanding, and while small incidents at nuclear weapons facilities are unlikely to start a war, they demonstrate a casual disregard for the dangers of the process.

**OPPOSITE** The universal sign indicating a risk from ionizing radiation – meaning radiation that carries sufficient energy to release electrons from atoms and molecules. The symbol first appeared in 1946 at the Berkeley Radiation Laboratory of the University of California. *(Warehouse Collection)*

**LEFT** In 1970, radioactive materials were accidentally released to the atmosphere from a 10-kiloton device detonated below the surface during the Baneberry Nuclear Test at the Nevada Test Site. Subsequent testing was suspended for six months following an investigation into the incident. *(US National Nuclear Security Administration)*

The first serious incident occurred within weeks of the bombs being used at Hiroshima and Nagasaki. On August 21, 1945, while working at the Los Alamos National Laboratory, Harry K. Daghlian Jr. dropped a tungsten-carbide brick on to a plutonium core, inadvertently creating a critical mass. Although he managed to retrieve the brick, he was fatally irradiated, dying three or four weeks later. Less than a year passed before Canadian physicist Louis Slotin, also at Los Alamos, manually assembled a critical mass of plutonium, accidentally causing a fission reaction which released a burst of radiation. He died, as did three of the ten who were watching.

An investigation into the safety of US nuclear weapons found that more than 1,000 safety-related incidents had occurred between 1950 and 1968. Many of the accidents were the result of simple carelessness, but there were several non-nuclear detonations of nuclear bombs as a result of aircraft accidents, with weapons damaged, set alight and lost during training exercises. In January 1961, for example, a B-52 Stratofortress on night patrol across the eastern seaboard of the USA accidentally dropped two hydrogen bombs over North Carolina, one falling in a field, the other into a tree; subsequent investigation showed that two out of the three safety switches had failed. In another notable episode, a dropped tool pierced the fuel tank of a "Titan 2" missile, resulting in an explosion that blew the missile's 9-megaton warhead 100 feet (30 m), fortunately without explosion.

And it wasn't just in the USA – more than 30 so-called "Broken Arrow" incidents have been reported between 1950 and 1980 where USAF aircraft accidentally dropped atomic weapons during training exercises. For example, in 1966, a USAF B-52 collided with a KC-135 tanker during an aerial refuelling operation over the south-east coast of Spain. Both aircraft were destroyed and the B-52 dropped its cargo of four 1.5-megaton bombs. Two were recovered intact, while the other two spread plutonium across more than 500 acres of Spanish countryside. The resulting clean-up cost the US government $80 million. Stories persist to this day that a fifth weapon remains in the Mediterranean leaking radioactive material into the environment.

Amidst a terrifying catalogue of bad luck, ineptitude and mechanical failure, however, the award for the most mundane accident goes to a group of Georgian soldiers, who, in 1997, suffered serious radiation poisoning and burns as a result of careless handling of training sources, including a caesium pellet that was found in the pocket of a shared jacket. The pellet was responsible for about 130,000 times the level of background radiation at a distance of 3 feet (1 m).

## Civilian accidents

The roll-call of civilian nuclear accidents is no less frightening. During a 60-year period there have been major incidents at Sellafield, Harrisburg, Chernobyl and Fukushima, as well as a series of accidents wherever there are nuclear power plants, including Argentina, Britain, Canada, France, Japan, the USA and the Soviet Union.

In the first civilian incident, at a generator plant at Chalk River, Ontario, the reactor core was damaged as a result of an event on December 12, 1952. Rated 5 on the 7-point International Nuclear Event Scale (INES), the incident did not result in widespread contamination, but the clean-up operation went on for two years, and involved more than 2,000 personnel.

There was a reactor fire at the British Sellafield plant (formerly Windscale) in 1957 that burned for three days, releasing radioactive material across Britain and Europe, and, in March 1979, at Three Mile Island, Pennsylvania,

**BELOW In April 1986, during a routine safety systems check of reactor number four at Chernobyl, a catastrophic explosion and fire released large amounts of radioactive particles into the atmosphere, spreading across much of the western USSR and Europe, with almost two-thirds of the fallout settling on Belarus.** *(Warehouse Collection)* a large amount of coolant escaped from the reactor core, resulting in a partial meltdown. Both of these incidents were rated INES 5. At Chernobyl in 1986, failures in the reactor safety system caused a steam explosion and subsequent meltdown of the reactor core. Rated INES 7, this incident released 400 times more radioactive material into the atmosphere than had resulted from the bombing of Hiroshima, with particles detected across Europe. There were approximately 50 fatalities as a direct result of the accident, and a huge area surrounding the plant remains quarantined. Finally, and also rated INES 7, the generator plant at Fukushima experienced partial meltdown of its reactors in 2011 following an earthquake and tsunami. Radioactive gases were deliberately released from two reactors to relieve pressure, while a series of explosions in all four of the reactor vessels caused a leakage of radioactive material.

The Fukushima accident changed attitudes to the safety of nuclear power. Within a year of the disaster, all but two of Japan's nuclear reactors had been shut down, Germany had announced that it would accelerate the closure of its nuclear plants and France agreed that it would reduce its reliance on nuclear power. In China, the government temporarily halted its nuclear power-station program, and, in Italy, 94% of the population voted against a government plan to build nuclear power stations.

# The bomb in popular culture

Not surprisingly, "the bomb" has made a significant impact on the public consciousness, featuring in films, novels, popular songs and art.

The first literary work to feature nuclear weapons was H.G. Wells's *The World Set Free*, dating from 1914, which described a technique for using the energy locked inside atomic particles to produce bombs. Cleve Cartmill predicted a chain-reaction nuclear bomb in his 1947 story *Deadline*, while Hugh Howey's 2011 *Silo* trilogy – *Wool*, *Shift* and *Dust* – is set in a world that has been deliberately destroyed by nuclear weapons in the belief that the inhabitants of the eponymous silos will, one day, emerge and establish a new order. In *The Turner Diaries*, written under a pseudonym by William Luther Pierce, the author imagines a revolution in the USA leading to nuclear war, and ultimately to a race war which sees many minority groups annihilated. Non-specific post-apocalypse scenarios also provide a popular setting for fiction, particularly those described as "pulp novels," with the reader left to imagine whether this has come about due to nuclear war, plague or some unnamed climatic disaster.

At the cinema, Stanley Kubrick's 1964 masterpiece, *Dr. Strangelove, or How I Learned to Stop Worrying and Love The Bomb*, used black humor and ridicule to great effect, while *The Atomic Café* (1982) wove a satirical narrative using clips from newsreels, TV news footage and US government-produced films. The *Planet of the Apes* series is set on a fictional earth ruled by apes following a disastrous nuclear war, while the 1990 film *By Dawn's Early Light* describes an accidental nuclear exchange following a "false flag" terrorist attack on the Soviet Union. Many of the James Bond films feature stolen or clandestine nuclear weapons.

And on television, the BBC's *War Game* drama-documentary of 1965 was banned for 20 years in Britain for its "horrifying effect," although it was shown to foreign audiences.

In 1983, ABC television produced a drama entitled *The Day After*, and a year later *Threads,* a television drama produced jointly by the BBC, Nine Network and Western-World Television, gave a chilling fictional account of nuclear war and its effects on Sheffield.

Many popular musicians have penned songs with an anti-nuclear-war theme, and many concerts have been held protesting both nuclear weapons and the use of nuclear power. On June 6, 1982, for example, a crowd of 85,000 gathered to listen to performers, including Bob Dylan, Crosby, Stills & Nash, Joan Baez and Stevie Wonder, performing in support of the UN Special Session on Nuclear

Disarmament. Less than a week later, a million people demonstrated in New York's Central Park against nuclear weapons, calling for an end to the arms race. Google brings up over 80 popular songs with an apocalyptic theme, including Tim Rose's "Come Away Melinda," "No Nuclear War" by Peter Tosh, "Manhattan Project" by Rush and "The Eve of Destruction" by Barry McGuire; others include Bob Dylan's "Masters of War" and "Talking World War Three Blues," "It's Good News Week" by Hedgehoppers Anonymous and Randy Newman's ironic "Political Science," which includes the immortal line "Let's drop the big one and see what happens." American satirist Tom Lehrer also wrote several songs with an anti-war theme, including "We Will All Go Together When We Go," while the lyrics to Sheldon Allman's 1960 song "Crawl Out Through the Fallout" can be found on YouTube.

In regard to art, even the most ardent anti-nuclear protestor would have to admit that a nuclear explosion is an awe-inspiring event, and it should be no surprise that artists have become obsessed with the imagery. As early as 1945, Salvador Dali produced a work entitled *Atomic and Uranian Melancholic Idyll* featuring decaying and molten objects. In 1950 the abstract painter Jackson Pollock tried to mimic the effects of a nuclear explosion, with paintings that released huge amounts of potential energy, and Andy Warhol produced a silkscreen entitled *Atomic Bomb*. Special mention should also be made of the New York-based artist Gregory Green, who constructs mock-ups of nuclear bombs in the style of "Little Boy."

## A nuclear-free future?

Whether or not it was right to use nuclear weapons in 1945 cannot easily be judged from the present day. Although it brought an end to the Second World War, a similar action today would almost certainly result in accusations of genocide and trials for crimes against humanity.

Tensions and mistrust still exist between East and West, but the old model in which opposing ideologies glared at one another across the Iron Curtain is history. Relations between the two sides have improved considerably since the darkest days of the Cold War, and a nuclear exchange between NATO and the Russian Federation seems unlikely. More recent nuclear powers, such as India and Pakistan, are content to believe they are adequately protected without the need to provoke their neighbors, and North Korea is probably discouraged from mounting a nuclear attack on its southern counterpart because of the uncertainty of the USA's reaction, and the size and scope of the US nuclear arsenal.

However, the technology cannot be uninvented, and, although multilateral disarmament would appear to be the best course, on the basis that all governments should instinctively be distrusted it is almost certain that a few weapons would be hidden "just in case." Currently, it seems that the balance of power actually serves as a deterrent. However, nuclear weapons have proliferated and other dangers have arisen: imagine nuclear technology falling into the hands of terrorist groups, or so-called

"rogue states" which have little to lose in any future conflict.

The world is not a safer place because of the existence of nuclear weapons – although perhaps it is safer than would be the case were these weapons only available to one nation.

**ABOVE** Preparation for an underground nuclear test at the Nevada Test Site in the 1990s. *(US National Nuclear Security Administration)*

**LEFT** On August 29, 1949, at the Soviet Semipalatinsk Test Site in Kazakhstan, the successful detonation of the 22-kiloton "First Lightning" – designated "Joe-1" by the Americans – broke the US monopoly on nuclear weapons and kick-started the nuclear arms race. *(TASS)*

# Glossary

**brinkmanship**   The practice of pushing a dangerous situation to the limit of safety, especially to force a certain outcome.

**Calvinism**   A set of Christian beliefs, based on the teachings of theologian John Calvin, that stresses God's power and the moral weakness of people.

**cataclysmic**   Relating to a violent or destructive event.

**clandestine**   Done in a private or secret way.

**disarmament**   The process of reducing the number of weapons controlled by a country's military.

**fission**   A process in which the nucleus of a heavy atom is split apart.

**fusion**   A process in which the nuclei of atoms are joined.

**half-life**   The time it takes for half the nuclei in a radioactive substance to spontaneously disintegrate.

**kerb**   British spelling of curb.

**MoD**   Ministry of Defence; the British government department responsible for defending and protecting the security of the United Kingdom.

**pitchblende**   A brown or black mineral form that consists of uraninite and contains radium.

**precipice**   A point where danger or difficulty begins.

**rem**   Roentgen equivalent man; a unit of radiation dosage equal to the amount of radiation that will cause the same biological effect as one rad of X-ray or gamma-ray exposure.

**roentgen**   A unit of x-radiation or gamma radiation equal to the amount of radiation that is produced in one cubic centimeter of dry air at 32°F (0°C); also used to describe something related to X-rays.

**stalemate**   A competition in which neither side can win or have the advantage.

**succour**   British spelling of succor, something done to help someone who is suffering or in a difficult situation.

# For More Information

The Cold War Museum
7142 Lineweaver Road
Warrenton, VA 20187
(540) 341-2008
Website: www.coldwar.org
The Cold War Museum is dedicated to educating the public on the global and political conflicts that occurred between East and West from the end of World War II to the dissolution of the Soviet Union. The museum also focuses on preservation and research of Cold War history.

The Diefenbunker
3929 Carp Road
Carp, Ontario K0A 1L0
Canada
(613) 839-0007
Website: www.diefenbunker.ca
Facebook and Twitter: @diefenbunker
YouTube: Diefenbunker Museum
The Diefenbunker was commissioned by Canadian Prime Minister John Diefenbaker in 1959 to house important members of the government and military in the event of a nuclear attack. Today a museum, the Diefenbunker, also called Canada's Cold War Museum, aims to increase the understanding and interest in Cold War history, both in Canada and internationally.

Subterranea Britannica
Heathend Cottage
Windsor Road
Ascot SL5 7LQ
England
Website: www.subbrit.org.uk
Subterranea Britannica is a UK-based society studying man-made underground structures and space, including nuclear bunkers. Many of the sites are comprehensively documented on the Society's website.

Titan Missile Museum
1580 W. Duval Mine Rd.
Sahuarita, Arizona 85629
(520) 625-7736
Website: www.titanmissilemuseum.org
Facebook: The Titan Missile Museum
The Titan Missile Museum is the only Titan II site that remains open to the public today. The museum is made up of two parts: the former missile site, now the Titan Missile National Historic Landmark, and the Count Ferdinand von Galen Titan Missile Museum Education and Research Center. The latter features a classroom, exhibit gallery, museum store and an archival storage area.

# For Further Reading

Allin, Dana H. *Cold War Illusions: America, Europe and Soviet Power 1969–1989*. New York, NY: St. Martin's Press, 1995.

Bougie, Matt. *Strategic Inventions of the Cold War*. New York, NY: Cavendish Square Publishing, 2016.

Byers, Ann. *The Legacy of the Cold War*. New York, NY: Cavendish Square Publishing, 2018.

Campbell, Duncan. *War Plan UK: The Truth about Civil Defence in Britain*. London, England: Burnett Books, 1982.

Catford, Nick. *Cold War Bunkers*. Wiltshire, England: Folly Books, 2010.

Clarke, Bob. *Britain's Cold War: The Dangerous Decades, An Illustrated History*. Stroud, England: Amberley Publishing, 2014.

Cocroft, Wayne D. and Roger J.C. Thomass. *Cold War: Building for Nuclear Confrontation 1946–1989*. Swindon, England: English Heritage, 2003.

Connolly, Kieron. *America's Bloody History from World War II to the Civil Rights Movement*. New York, NY: Enslow Publishing, 2017.

Duling, Kaitlyn. *Nuclear Proliferation, the Military-Industrial Complex, and the Arms Race*. New York, NY: Cavendish Square Publishing, 2018.

George, Enzo. *The Cold War*. New York, NY: Cavendish Square Publishing, 2016

Grant, Matthew. *After the Bomb: Civil Defence and Nuclear War in Britain 1945–68*. New York, NY: Palgrave Macmillan, 2010.

McCamley, Nick. *Cold War Secret Nuclear Bunkers: The Passive Defence of the Western World during the Cold War*. Barnsley, England: Pen & Sword Military, 2013.

Siracusa, Joseph M. *Nuclear Weapons: A Very Short Introduction*. New York, NY: Oxford University Press, 2008.

Young-Brown, Fiona. *Nuclear Fusion and Fission*. New York, NY: Cavendish Square, 2017.

Younger, Stephen M. *The Bomb: A New History*. New York, NY: Ecco Press, 2009.

# Index